Recommendations for "Career Suicide is Overrated"

"'Career Suicide' is a must have, must read book for any leader in the public safety world. The real-life examples provided from an author who has "walked the walk" puts everyday leadership into the grasp of all current and aspiring leaders. This book should be on the desk or in the duty bag of every public safety leader. I only wish such a comprehensive guidebook on leadership that focuses on the mental well-being of our employees was available earlier in my career."

-Rick Derus
Deputy Chief, Windsor Police (Ret'd)

"Brian's latest book is an incredibly honest perspective that anyone in a position of leadership needs to read. It is extremely difficult for a Leader to understand PTS if they have never experienced it. Brian's book offers Leaders very pragmatic ideas that, if utilized, will assure a culture of compassion and adaptation."

-Kelly Donovan
President, Fit4Duty - The Ethical Standard

"Brian Knowler is a leader in many ways - this book shines a bright light on this fact. Being a good leader is not easy, thankfully this book highlights ways to be such, and encourages the implementation of new techniques to foster positive direction and management."

-Natalie Harris, BHSc, AEMCA, ACP
Founder of Wings of Change Peer Support
City Councillor – Barrie, Ontario

"Very well written and packed with insight from the perspective of one who has been there and seen both the dark and light side of leadership in a PTS world. Works like Brian's represent the next big step in emergency services leadership."

-Training Officer Mike McFadden
Calgary Fire Service

"In Brian's latest book he once again opens himself up, so that others can benefit. Brian shares personal stories and anecdotes that emphasise key modern leadership concepts that are absolutely essential. Most importantly Brian outlines how leaders need to be caring, understanding and supportive, but ties these lessons to the factors that affect those with Post Traumatic Stress. This should be essential reading for front line (Capital-L) Leaders that are entrusted with supporting staff with demanding roles."

-Scott Ramey
Division Chief, Halifax Regional Fire and Emergency Services

"Fills a very necessary gap in how Leaders should deal with those that suffer from not just PTS but any OSI...I could very easily relate to everything Brian wrote as a spouse, as a retired military member and as a Leader. Brian's book is the most accurate description of what a Leader needs to portray if the stigma around mental health issues is to be broken. This book needs to be read and on the desk of every Leader no matter the occupation."

-Captain (Ret'd) Carrie Pluck, CD
Canadian Armed Forces
Co-Founder Ensinger Acres Equine Therapy

"Insightful. Packed with hard-won wisdom. Brian lays his soul bare in his quest to make us all better Leaders. This book will change lives!!"

-LTCOL(Ret'd) Kyle Tyrrell, MBA, PSC(j)
Australian Army Combat Veteran, PTS Survivor,
Leadership Consultant
CEO Vanguard Global Security and Risk Management

"This book fills a critical gap in current leadership and mental health literature. In a short volume, Brian Knowler covers it all --ethics, leadership vs. management, even trying to keep the game face on at work when you're barely keeping it together inside. Speaking as a manager who's dealt with my own anxiety issues and having seen them in my co-workers, this book should be on every leader's must-read list."

-Tim Campbell, Division Head
City of Fullerton, CA

"Brian's book was a raw and honest account of all he's experienced... I can completely appreciate and respect his characterization of leadership (including Capital L Leadership). Brian's book resonated with me deeply. Both as the Leader I continually strive to be and as a mental health professional. It is a wonderful piece of work that will undoubtedly touch many and influence change!"

-Veronica Felizardo
Registered Social Worker and Psychotherapist
Canada Border Services Agency

"I am a nurse who is now a new manager, who has worked in healthcare for over 30 years and has personally experienced some traumatic incidents during my career. Brian's book has wonderful advice, as if he were speaking directly to me! It will help me support my staff when critical incidents happen, as well as with the day-to-day issues managers and staff face together. It reminded me to remember to take care of myself, because I matter as well as my staff."

-Gail Slack, RN, BScN, MSN
Unit Manager, Chatham-Kent Health Alliance

"This book is an essential read for all Managers. It ties management principles with mental health principles in a way that clarifies each is dependent on the other. I can't wait to see it out there as it is a key set of messages for Managers, not just in Emergency Services."

-Bernie Tighem, BAppB:ES, CFO
Manager Technical and Field Services
Lakeland Emergency Training Centre

"Brian Knowler's new book is a terrific look into the difference between "Managers and Leaders". Not only from the purest standpoint, but from a perspective of understanding the impact of PTS and what true leaders might consider when dealing with persons impacted by this debilitating injury. Through Brian's book and well-presented personal experiences, he is assisting the first responder world, and leadership within that world to quickly make up time and space in getting to where it needs to be so that trauma will cease to claim so many."

-Lt Col (Ret'd) Chris Linford, CD, BScN
Wounded Warriors Canada National Ambassador
Author of 'Warrior Rising'

"People in leadership positions can greatly impact the lives of those they lead – positively or negatively. Within the PTS realm, knowing their people and recognizing the need to support them while maintaining open and trusting relationships, will allow true leaders to do all they can to help them following life-altering one-time traumatic incidents or careers filled with cumulative negative experiences.

Brian has been on both sides of the PTS world – as a leader and as an employee suffering from it. Thankfully, he emerged from his personal crisis healthy and caring, and once again presents his valuable thoughts, theories and lessons-learned very well in his latest book. It's a must-read for all levels within the emergency services sector."

-Chris Lewis
OPP Commissioner (Ret'd)
President, Lighthouse Leadership Services
Author of 'Never Stop on a Hill'

CAREER SUICIDE IS OVERRATED

EQUIPPING LEADERS WITH MENTAL HEALTH STRATEGIES FOR THEIR TEAMS AND THEMSELVES

INCLUDES COVID LEADERSHIP LESSONS

BRIAN KNOWLER

Career Suicide Is Overrated
Copyright © 2021 by Brian Knowler. All rights reserved.

Published by Author Academy Elite
PO Box 43, Powell, OH 43065
www.AuthorAcademyElite.com

All rights reserved. This book contains material protected under international and federal copyright laws and treaties. Any unauthorized reprint or use of this material is prohibited. No part of this book may be reproduced or transmitted in any form or by any means, electronic or mechanical, including photocopying, recording, or by any information storage and retrieval system, without express written permission from the author.

Identifiers:

Library of Congress Control Number: 2021911835

ISBN: 978-1-64746-836-1 (paperback)
ISBN: 978-1-64746-837-8 (hardback)
ISBN: 978-1-64746-838-5 (ebook)

Available in paperback, hardback, ebook, & audiobook

Any Internet addresses (websites, blogs, etc.) and telephone numbers printed in this book are offered as a resource. They are not intended in any way to be or imply an endorsement by Author Academy Elite, nor does Author Academy Elite vouch for the content of these sites and numbers for the life of this book

First Printing: 2021

455 Victoria Ave, Chatham, ON, N7L 3B4

www.brianknowler.com

To Cathy, Jack, and Brady. You're still my heroes.

Preface and Acknowledgements

In March of 2016, I published my first book, 'On the Other Side of Broken – One Cop's Battle With the Demons of PTS.' It detailed my journey through PTS up to that point, starting with the on-duty critical incident that I experienced, through my growing isolation and downward spiral, my crash in early 2012, my journey back to becoming the 'old Brian' I had been, and, finally, experiencing post-traumatic growth.

The first paragraph of the last chapter of 'On the Other Side…" reads:

"And with that, my work comes to a close. Or, at least, this written work. I like to think that my real work is just beginning. After all, PTS is a journey that never really ends. It just has moments of quiet and calm during what can otherwise be a stormy time. The demon can be tamed, but it will always be there, just under the surface."

Since releasing that book, and the first edition of the one in your hands, the 'real work' I alluded to has included speaking to conferences, emergency services, non-profits, hospitals, symposiums, and campuses on topics around operational stress injuries and first responders.

I've appeared on TV and radio talk shows, podcasts, and webinars.

I created a mental health and Leadership program to accompany the material in the book and won an international award for Excellence in Mental Health for it.

I regained a rank in my career, but also took a good chunk of time off to get myself re-balanced and well after feeling the roller coaster of PTS start to climb very quickly up a long hill.

But I wanted to do more. I wanted to start shaping a culture that I've been part of for over twenty years; to help direct up and coming Leaders who will replace my generation within a few years and who hopefully will view mental health issues in first responders as just another injury that is acknowledged, treated, accommodated, and considered a mark of courage, not one of shame.

I just wasn't sure how to do it. But then, as it often does, the universe opened a door for me.

The origin of this book lies in a conversation I had with retired Ontario Provincial Police Commissioner Chris Lewis (lighthouseleadershipservices.com.) Chris was speaking at a leadership conference I attended and was the final speaker on the first day of the conference. Chris continues, even in retirement, to be a strong advocate for improving leadership and for issues around psychological health and wellness in policing. I had a chance that day to pick up a copy of his excellent book 'Never Stop on a Hill' and, after hours, had a chat with him over a few pints.

The topic of PTS and leadership came up while we were chatting. Chris very kindly complimented me on my first book and then asked if I thought that PTS had changed how I made decisions as a leader. After a few sips and some contemplation, my answer was 'I don't see how it couldn't have'.

As I've learned through many interactions with Chris, he wasn't content to let that go. He pushed me for some details, I think as much to make sure I knew for myself as to answer him. As the conversation went on, we both came to the same points – those traumatic events had changed us both as police officers, that it changed our leadership styles for the better (I'll expand on this in a later section of the book,) and that as our careers have progressed, we both became more and more cognizant of the emotional and psychological toll 'the job' takes on those in uniform. That led to a quiet toast to some fallen comrades, a handshake, and Chris moved on to another group for a new conversation.

As he walked away, I realized that I had just had a lesson in what I will be calling 'Capital-L' Leadership. I'll use that term to differentiate between regular leaders (and anyone who is a 'leader' as opposed to a 'manager' is already light years ahead in their ability to influence people,) and those who, through their Leadership style, believe and live what I'll be discussing in this book.

This is by no means an exhaustive work on leadership, trauma, mental health, or anything else. The book is full of pieces of wisdom I've picked up; the collected observations of someone who has spent almost a decade fighting his own demons and helping others fight theirs, has a bit of talent at writing, and has had the love and support of many people to continue doing all these things. Wherever possible, I've illustrated each point with an anecdote from my own experience or that of someone close to me that I've been made privy too. I use no names or work locations as I want the anecdotes to illustrate the point, not cast blame. I also have drawn on the hundreds of conversations, interviews, and meetings I've had with first responders and frontline workers across the world about their experiences, both good and bad, as they moved through their PTS journeys.

Anyone who has ever done any reading on leadership will have rapidly come to realize that there have been reams of material written on the topic; more than one could ever absorb in a lifetime. Countless thinkers and intellectuals have left their wisdom for us to follow, and I've turned to them to help illustrate my points. For each section of the book, I've included two quotes. Being a history geek, in each instance I've attempted to include a quote from a classical source – Greek, Roman, Latin, and Renaissance Europe – as well as a more modern one. Wisdom comes in all forms, and far be it from me to argue against standing on the shoulders of giants.

Plato said, "Those who tell the stories rule society." As a storyteller, I don't want to rule society…I just want to nudge it a bit. Small actions that impact many people create massive change.

ONE VERY IMPORTANT NOTE – NOTHING IN THIS BOOK OR ANY OF THE SUGGESTED WEBSITES OR READING IS A SUBSTITUTE FOR PROFESSIONAL HELP. IF YOU ARE EXPERIENCING A MENTAL HEALTH CRISIS OR THINK YOU ARE DEALING WITH A MENTAL HEALTH ISSUE, CONTACT YOUR PHYSICIAN, A LOCAL EMERGENCY ROOM OR CRISIS CENTRE; OR CALL ONE OF THE MANY REAL-TIME CRISIS LINES WHERE TRAINED COUNSELORS WILL WORK WITH YOU.

Acknowledgements and Thanks

First and foremost, to my wife Cathy and my sons Brady and Jack, who put up with late nights at the computer, cursing coming from the office, technical questions, and being endlessly sought out for opinions on design, colours, and wording. I love you all.

To my mom and dad, both of whom saw their circumstances change drastically since my first book was published. My dad died in June 2017 after a lengthy battle with liver issues and my mom had a stroke and heart attack shortly after that. Thank you for reminding me that life is fragile and can change in a heartbeat.

Thank you to my editors and early readers: Alysson Storey, Todd Humber, and Jason MacKenzie.

To my endorsers and early reviewers: my humble, eternal thanks.

To Leigh-Ann Closs Smith, who sadly died far too young from cancer as this book was being finalized. Godspeed Leigh, and thank you for your early notes and ideas as this book was taking shape. You were a great inspiration, a great friend, and a great first crush back in Grade 9.

To all the public safety personnel who supported my first book, who made me see that the ups and downs of a decade were not limited to me alone, and who encouraged me to keep writing about something that has taken so many of our brothers and sisters.

To Veronica Felizardo and Bernie Tighem, who not only wrote wonderful endorsements but provided me with 11th-hour angles to the book I hadn't really thought of, prompting a frenzied but appreciated re-write.

To those officers and support personnel I have had the honour to lead – thank you for letting me experiment, fail, laugh, adapt, brainstorm, think, and grow as a leader.

To the men of SAW Cohort 087, November 2019. Thank you. I never had a brother growing up, but I have a bunch of new ones now.

Finally, to the brothers and sisters on the frontlines who have lost their battle, for whatever reason. You are not forgotten, and you are never alone. *Requiescant in pace.*

Introduction

In October of 2004, I experienced my first major traumatic incident as a police officer. I had been to homicides, gruesome vehicle collisions, violent sexual assaults, drownings, industrial accidents, a plane crash, even the evacuation of a town due to an industrial fire – all reasonably the run of the mill, but still unsettling – events that police officers attend to as part of their duties. But that October night in 2004 was something different entirely. That night, I watched a good friend who had been battered in a rollover collision die in my arms while being unable to do anything about it. I tried to open up to a senior officer who was supposed to be a mentor and was soundly rebuffed in my efforts to try to talk to him about the impact this death had on me. I gave up trying to talk about it after that.

My friend Mike died, I thought I handled it properly, and life went on to include transfers and promotions and a rapid rise through the ranks as a young, promising leader. I handled it myself, without needing anyone else, without confiding in anyone else. I handled it like a cop should, I thought.

I was wrong. Completely, utterly wrong.

As the years after Mike's death went on, cracks began to form across the fabric of my life. In my demeanour. In my marriage. In my status as a dad. In the foundations of my career. I began to live dangerously, taking risks with my job and marriage, often not caring, and giving myself over to the loss of control, the chaos, and the web of lies and half-truths I started to find myself in.

I started finding solace in the bottle, and for a few months at the end of 2011 alcohol was my coping mechanism, my escape, and my sleeping pill. I was spiraling downwards rapidly, and not even a move across the province that was going to be good for both family and work could make a difference. It was a dark, sad, horrible time that I look back on with very few fond memories; a time that I lost as a dad, husband, and friend. A time that I will never get back.

The thing about downward spirals is that, inevitably, they must end. Mine ended on a cold January night in 2012 in a tangle of tears, regret, remorse, and despair that I only managed to pull through due to much stronger people than I picking me up, pointing me in the direction of a path that led to healing, and holding my hand along the way. They led me when I couldn't lead myself.

As I began my journey of healing and redemption, leadership, or lack thereof, would become a keystone of my recovery. I mean that both in terms of leaders who had an impact on me, either helpful or harmful, as well as in how I carried myself as a leader with my newfound knowledge and status as 'a cop with PTS.'

In the first few months after starting therapy, life was more about restoring balance and survival than growth or self-discovery. However, after I could get back to at least some of the man I had been before so completely and utterly falling, I began to take notice of the subtle ways that the leaders around me were influencing my post-traumatic growth.

In turn, I was also finding an outlet for expressing elements of this journey back from blackness through writing, speaking, and opening myself up to other first responders who were going through the same thing and needed to know that they weren't alone. I also found kindred spirits in other uniforms of all stripes who felt the same way I did when it came to living out loud – we all felt first responder PTS was something to be talked about, something to be dragged from the shadows, and something to be faced down.

But not everyone agreed.

Even nine short years ago I met with resistance when it came to the frank and open way I discussed what had happened, and what was continuing to happen, to me. I was told that I was damaging my career, that I was labelling myself as broken, that psychological injuries in the first responder field should stay quiet and hidden and behind a wall. And this was by people who were supposedly leaders in their respective fields and organizations! I sometimes despaired at this and wondered how the frontline personnel, the ones who really needed to be educated and empowered and know that it was okay to talk about this, would ever get the message filtered down to them from these kinds of so-called leaders.

I've seen both sides of the coin these past six years. The bad leaders have done little to nothing for the cause; the good leaders have stepped up to support and showed they understand the stakes that first responders are facing when it comes to their psychological health.

This might be an ideal time to review the whole concept of manager/boss vs leader. There are literally hundreds of scholarly works comparing the two; I've read many of them and distilled them down to a simple 10-item list:

MANAGER / BOSS	*LEADER*
-Drives others	-Coaches others
-Inspires fear	-Inspires enthusiasm

-Blames others	-Helps fix the problem
-Says "I"	-Says "We"
-Knows how it's done	-Shows how it's done
-Depends on authority for compliance	-Depends on goodwill for compliance
-Uses people	-Develops people
-Takes credit	-Gives credit
-Commands	-Asks
-Says "Go!"	-Says "Let's go!"

Hopefully, since you're reading this book, your goal is to be a leader, not a manager.

And, ideally, you want to be the best leader possible…

These are what I refer to as Capital-L Leaders. These are leaders who, through word, thought, and deed, move past managers, move past leaders, and become something else altogether – an individual who understands that, when you lead people, they are your ultimate asset. Capital-L Leaders have grasped the concept that employee health, wellness, harmony, and security must come first when you lead people. In doing this, you create a stronger, more resilient workplace with higher morale, higher productivity, and higher attendance. Study after study has shown this. Your bottom line should always be your people.

(Throughout the book, I'll denote when I'm referring to this concept by using the term 'Leader', or, if at the start of a sentence, 'Capital-L Leader'.)

The CAPITAL-L Leadership program I designed in conjunction with the 2nd edition of this book takes as its foundation the following leadership tools, all discussed in the book:

C – Communication
A – Self-Awareness
P – Perception
I – No One Is An Island
T – Teams Are The Foundation

A – Admit Mistakes
L – Live Out Loud
L – Leave A Trail

How does this tie into this book, you ask? A fair question. Simply put, I'll be recounting lessons in both leadership and Leadership (and, sometimes, management,) that I've learned in the thirteen years since my friend Mike died next to me in the wreckage of his minivan. Most of the lessons will relate in one form or another to mental health issues.

Due to my own PTS, I've been immersed more than many others in this world of mental health in the workplace. I've navigated making a workplace injury claim, had to deal with telling my supervisors and peers about my condition, fought through the tangle of paperwork for benefits and treatment, and struggled through going to the office on days I didn't think I'd be able to get out of bed.

This is an area, that, to be blunt, anyone who is aspiring to a leadership role can no longer ignore. Issues around mental health and wellness are inescapable in today's world – employee well-being, media, risk management, health and safety protocols, corporate liability, sick time, medical plan premiums, modified work planning, employee retention, training.... There's virtually no facet of modern work life that isn't impacted by mental health concerns.

I've always been fascinated by leadership as a concept and since I was a kid, I've always strived to put myself into positions of leadership. I found the idea of influencing people with the pull of your personality a fascinating one and started reading about the subject before I hit my teens, in both classical works and modern books.

I was a Scout for many years and achieved the highest award possible in that organization, Chief Scout. When I was sixteen, I was voted my hometown's Junior Citizen of the Year. I was involved with student government at my high school and university. Also in university, I was the student director of the freshman orientation program and a peer mentor. In law school, I was on several committees and at graduation was awarded the John Whiteside Award, which is given in recognition of a student's contributions to faculty, community, and leadership. When I went to Police College, I was asked to represent my class for the valedictorian competition.

Once I started my policing career, I moved quickly through the ranks and at one point was one of the youngest, if not the youngest, officers at the rank of Inspector in the province of Ontario. I'm also in a unique position in that since I was diagnosed with PTS, I have always been in positions of leadership; first at the middle level of my organization, and then, by my choice, on a smaller unit level. I've been able to juggle these two worlds, leadership and mental health, usually successfully, sometimes with some spectacular fails. I've also been privy to some stunning mistakes by other leaders, as well as some amazing successes in this area.

I don't lay these achievements out to brag, but I do want to establish my credibility as a leader. I've made a conscious effort to walk the talk as laid out in the book, and I've received enough positive feedback through commendations, performance evaluations, awards, and messaging that I feel confident in knowledgeably talking about the highs, and lows, of being a leader.

I'm sure there are many out there who will disagree with my basic axiom: that employees should come first and that if they do you will be the better for it. It boggles me that there are still those in positions of authority who feel this way, but human nature is what it is, and some will always view people as expendable assets who can simply be replaced when they wear out or break. For far too long, especially in the first responder world, that was the prevailing mindset, and one that has damaged or destroyed countless lives.

Those who wish to lead can no longer subscribe to that mindset.

It's the Capital-L leaders I've had the fortune to know who, over the last nine years, have helped shepherd me back to a place of light and love and who have helped change minds and hearts across the first responder community, and the public at large, about post-traumatic stress and psychological well-being.

But that's a topic to discuss in the Conclusion. On with the show.

Brain Basics

The human brain is an infinitely fascinating machine. It runs on bioelectricity, it doesn't feel pain, it actively works to protect you from the worst experiences and memories of your life, and it can rewire its neuro-chemical pathways to go around damaged areas. A remarkable construct.

A full writeup of the mechanics of the brain would fill several dozen of these pages. My intent is to give you a very basic overview of how brain function may impact your role as a Leader, as explained to me by a team of trauma counselors.

Your brain can be split into three 'smaller brains' that control your day-to-day behaviour:

-The Lizard Brain – controls your fight or flight response, concerned with your survival.

-The Limbic Brain – controls your emotions, creates memories, senses pleasure.

-The Cortex – the logic centre, assists with planning and anticipation, controls reasoning.

In a regular person, these three facets will be (more or less) equally in control. Obviously, not everyone is the same –genetic and biological differences in how these three brains function are what create the extraordinary and unique individuals who inhabit society.

One of the keys as a Leader is to figure out when dealing with someone what their 'brain' is. Are they more driven by emotion or logic? Will they respond more strongly to statistics or to a human-interest angle? If you can figure out what approach will best work, you will go a long way towards better being able to bridge the gaps between you, which, after all, is the point of communication.

This can even vary by gender. Commonly, men are more apt to focus on a problem-solving strategy that is more rational or logical, focusing on the problem itself. Women, generally, will be more emotionally focused and look more at the human factor when problem-solving. (The 'Men Are from Mars, Women Are from Venus' theory.)

PLEASE REMEMBER THE ABOVE IS ONLY A GUIDELINE!!!

Ideally, Leaders will be able to strike a balance between problem-focused and emotion-focused strategies when they are going through their day-to-day routines. Keep in mind that situational leadership will often not allow for the luxury of internally debating all sides of an issue.

The fact that the limbic system is one of your 'little brains' is the reason that Leaders need to have strong emotional intelligence, which is the ability to recognize their own emotions and those of others and to manage and use those emotions for constructive purposes. You can't turn your emotions off, no matter how much you may want to at times, and a substantial part of Leadership is striking that balance between letting your emotions ground your decisions and letting them run roughshod over you. It can be a fine balance at times but mastery of it is key to effective Leadership.

> "I consider that a man's brain originally is like a little empty attic, and you have to stock it with such furniture as you choose."
> -ARTHUR CONAN DOYLE, ENGLISH SHORT STORY WRITER AND NOVELIST; CREATOR OF SHERLOCK HOLMES

> "The brain is a complex biological organ of great computational capability that constructs our sensory experiences, regulates our thoughts and emotions, and control our actions."
> – ERIC KANDEL, AUSTRIAN-AMERICAN NEUROSCIENTIST; PROFESSOR OF BIOCHEMISTRY AND BIOPHYSICS; NOBEL PRIZE WINNER

Enter Post-Traumatic Stress

Something that Leaders would do well to keep in mind – PTS disrupts the linkages between the three brains! Someone with PTS is very often in fight or flight mode, which means their lizard brain is dominating the other two. Because of this, there are very specific treatments for trauma that take that fact into account and work to reduce the grip that the lizard brain has on the person.

Unlike simple stress, trauma changes your perspectives. It shatters your most basic assumptions about yourself and how you used to see the world.

"Life is good," "I'm safe," "People are kind," "I can trust others," "The future is likely to be good" are representative of what most people would consider to be positive feelings about their place in the world.

PTS replaces them with feelings like "The world is dangerous," "I can't win," "I can't trust other people," or "There's no hope." Because of this, communication and bridge-building can become extremely difficult.

As a Leader, there are ways to speak to someone with PTS that will be more effective and help create understanding on both sides of the conversation:

-If you haven't already, educate yourself about PTS and other operational stress injuries – Leaders can't afford to ignore this aspect of their role any longer.

-Don't assume someone with PTS is mentally weak or psychologically unstable.

-Keep boundaries, both physical and psychological, in mind (i.e., personal space, touching the person).

-If the person is feeling triggered, simply ask what you can do to help. Unless you're a trained therapist or asked by the person, don't offer suggestions or opinions.

-Speak softly in a moderated tone of voice (helps avoid the startle reflex many with PTS have).

-The person may not want to talk about what's bothering them, but that doesn't mean they aren't suffering at the time.

-Put aside your own perceptions and remember that trauma is this person's reality.

-Don't minimize the person's feelings or say you understand if you don't really understand.

-Everyone has different coping mechanisms. Accept that. If someone needs to lie on the floor for ten minutes to ground themselves, roll with it and offer them space and support.

-Remember that the person's current reactions are not about the present, but about what happened in their past.

-Believe them.

-Listen. Just, listen.

There are also the moral injury components of PTS to consider. Moral injury occurs when a person is involved in or witnesses an act that impacts them on a deep human level. This is different from the neurological impact of a traumatic event; a moral injury is something that hits you in a place where your spirit, soul, culture, and psyche live. Moral injuries can be extremely debilitating and are generally treated during PTS therapy. Most often, moral injury manifests itself in anger, shame, unnecessary guilt, and social alienation. It's not difficult to see how these aspects of PTS can be incredibly impactful.

During interviews of first responders for my previous book, the concept of moral injury came up often. Frequent examples included officer-involved shootings, failing to save a life or successfully perform first aid, feeling like one's co-workers or partners have been let down by something the first responder did (or didn't) do, and arriving at a call too late to be of assistance in possibly preventing a tragic outcome.

These interviews hit home for me. I certainly experienced moral injury with Mike's death. My job is to help preserve life. I showed up at a scene where life needed to be preserved. I didn't do my job properly, and because of that, someone I knew died. I failed.

For seven years, that's how I felt. I was wrong.

I did some excellent reflecting, writing, and meditating on this during my treatment, all guided by my doctor, who was an amazing Leader in her own right. Through these activities, I came to realize that for years, I had been extremely hard on myself, unfairly so. There was nothing more I could have done; I did what I was able to with what I had at my disposal. I did my job, and I did my best. Sometimes, life just throws curveballs at you.

Unfortunately, in my case, this was a curveball that derailed me for years; but one that my doctor, a trained, caring, compassionate Leader, helped me overcome. My ongoing hope is that I can help others the same way and pay things forward.

> **"Healing is a matter of time, but it is also sometimes a matter of opportunity."**
>
> -HIPPOCRATES, 4ᵀᴴ CENTURY BC GREEK PHYSICIAN AND PHILOSOPHER; CONSIDERED ONE OF THE MOST OUTSTANDING FIGURES IN THE HISTORY OF THE MEDICAL ARTS; OFTEN REFERRED TO AS THE "FATHER OF MEDICINE"

> **"Traumatic events challenge an individual's view of the world as a just, safe and predictable place. Traumas that are caused by human behavior... commonly have more psychological impact than those caused by nature."**
>
> -AMERICAN PSYCHOLOGICAL ASSOCIATION, FROM THE APA DICTIONARY OF PSYCHOLOGY

Armor Isn't Just for Knights – The Importance of Building Resilience

'**R**esilience' is a term that gets thrown around extensively when it comes to mental health issues. What does it really mean?

One could easily fill a complete book with the concepts of resilience. For our much simpler and streamlined purposes, resilience means this: it's the ability to successfully cope with a crisis and to return to your pre-crisis status quickly.

You put resilience into practice when you use mental processes and behaviors you've learned to protect yourself from the potential negative effects of stressors. Or, conversely, if you haven't built up those mental shields to protect yourself, you potentially let stressors overwhelm you. That overwhelm could be temporary or longer-term. Just like every trauma is relative, so is every moment of overwhelm.

One of my favourite all time songs illustrates this point much more poetically than I ever could. Despite the melancholy nature of the lyrics, during the first few verses of 'Hasn't Hit Me Yet' by Blue Rodeo, the narrator demonstrates considerable resilience in the face of losing someone he clearly loves immensely. It's a fantastic song, a classic that for Canadians of a certain vintage evokes both memories of summer (the album came out in July of 1993) and winter (the breakup in the song takes place while snow is falling on Lake Ontario.) Give it a listen if you don't know it.

Obviously, building resilience is what leaders want not only for those they lead, but themselves. Resilience can be learned and improved, just like any other skill. The amazing thing is that there are as many ways to build your resilience as there are Leaders. Here are just a simple few; the key is that it must be something that hits YOU, that impacts YOU. You can't wear someone else's armor without having some spots that aren't protected (a couple of these points will be repeated throughout the book and be recurring themes.)

-Educate yourself about resilience through research, reading, and talking to mental health professionals.

-Practice self-care. Practice self-care. Practice self-care.

-Don't compare yourself to others. You are an individual and what protects you won't match to anyone else.

-Never assume you can do it all, and don't be afraid to ask for help.

-Breathe. Lots.

-Compassion is a powerful tool. Practice it often and you'll reap the benefits when you need it yourself.

-Draw boundaries and ensure that you keep the right people in and out of those boundaries.

-Remove toxic people and things from your life; they simply sap your strength and serve as a frustration.

-Celebrate the small, daily victories to remind yourself of the good you're doing in the world – they'll fuel you when life starts to look ugly.

-Have a happy place, either mental or literal. Make it your own, surround yourself with things that bring you happiness and remind you of who you truly are, and visit there often.

-Capital-L Leaders network and connect with others for a reason. Build up a strong support network of people you know you can go to when you can't do it all on your own.

-Never stop growing. Never stop learning. The person who thinks they know everything they will ever need to know has already lost half the battle.

Obviously, this is but a smattering of physical and mental activities you can undertake to increase your resilience. Experiment, communicate, tinker until you have in place what works for you. It's not a one-and-done; you will always need resilience and there will be times that you must reach down deep into the well and use up every drop you have.

"Fall seven times, stand up eight."
-AUTHOR UNKNOWN, FEUDAL-ERA JAPAN

"Resilience is the ability to attack while running away."

-Wes Fesler, three-sport athlete at Ohio State (football, basketball, baseball); later went on to successful coaching careers in college football and basketball; member of College Football Hall of Fame

Support Your Team...

It's very easy to support your people and Lead them when things are going smoothly. However, Leadership doesn't stop when the good times do. It is extremely important that you support your people even when times are bad and it's not easy to do so. In fact, that's the most critical time – it's during moments of chaos that your people will look for a Leader. This is your opportunity to step up and be the one they find.

Just after my PTS diagnosis, my brand-new supervisor, who barely knew me, immediately offered encouragement and workplace accommodation if I needed it when I told her what was happening. When I published my first book, a previous supervisor got in touch with me over ten years since I last worked for him and apologized for, in his words, 'missing the fact that you were hurting'.

In my case, either of these Leaders could have simply ignored the circumstances amid the million other things they had on their minds. But they didn't, and what they did became a part of my journey of healing I will always look back on with fondness and gratitude.

> *"Molon Labe"* "Come and take them."
> -KING LEONIDAS OF SPARTA, 5ᵀᴴ CENTURY BC; SAID BY LEONIDAS WHEN THE SPARTANS WERE TOLD TO LAY DOWN THEIR WEAPONS AS HE STOOD AT THE HEAD OF HIS FAR-OUTNUMBERED TROOPS FACING DOWN THE PERSIAN ARMY AT THERMOPYLAE

> **"When you're part of a team, you stand up for your teammates. Your loyalty is to them. You protect them through good and bad because they'd do the same for you."**
> -YOGI BERRA, LEGENDARY NEW YORK YANKEES PLAYER, MANAGER, AND COACH

...And Know Your Team

Along with supporting your team, this is another foundation of Leadership: know your team. In small teams, this is easy. In large teams, you need to trust your small-team Leaders to keep you informed. Knowing your people and having that close-knit communication (the value of communication of all types to a Leader can never be over-rated!) will let you know when they are not themselves – when they're having a difficult day, when their work is off, and, ultimately, when they are in crisis and struggling. Sometimes the smallest clue will give you massive insight – if you're watching for it and are ready to take the steps needed to help them through that crisis.

Having to approach someone when they are in crisis can be very, very tricky, but Leadership isn't about taking the easy path. Later in the book, I talk about difficult conversations and the whys and wherefores of initiating them. This is a skill which I would urge you to practice whenever you get the opportunity.

"To know, is to know that you know nothing. That is the meaning of true knowledge."

-SOCRATES, 3ʳᴰ CENTURY BC GREEK PHILOSOPHER; ONE OF THE FOUNDERS OF WESTERN PHILOSOPHY; THE FIRST MORAL PHILOSOPHER; ORIGINATOR OF THE 'SOCRATIC METHOD' OF LEARNING

"The day the soldiers stop bringing you their problems is the day you stopped leading them. They have either lost confidence that you can help them or concluded that you don't care. Either case is a failure of leadership."

-GENERAL COLIN POWELL, AMERICAN ELDER STATESMAN; RETIRED FOUR-STAR GENERAL; NATIONAL SECURITY ADVISOR; COMMANDER OF THE U.S. ARMY FORCES COMMAND DURING 90/91 GULF WAR; FIRST AFRICAN AMERICAN TO SERVE AS CHAIRMAN OF THE JOINT CHIEFS OF STAFF AND SECRETARY OF STATE

Live Out Loud (See also" 'Career Suicide' is Overrated"' later in the book.)

Never be afraid to live out loud. Some of the most inspiring moments of your life can come from when you say, 'to hell with it', take a deep breath, and do something publicly that terrifies you, especially if you aren't completely sure if you should.

In 2012, I told my story in the most public way possible. I composed a message to my entire office telling my PTS story from start to finish. The ten seconds before I hit 'Send' on that message to publicly tell my story for the first time were the longest ten seconds of my life, but ultimately led to some of the greatest and most redeeming experiences I've ever had.

You never know who or what your example will inspire.

"The risk of a wrong decision is preferable to the terror of indecision."

-MAIMONIDES, 12TH CENTURY EGYPTIAN RABBI, SCHOLAR, AND WRITER

"Dream up the kind of world you want to live in. Dream out loud."

-BONO, LEAD SINGER OF U2; WINNER OF 22 GRAMMY AWARDS; MEMBER OF ROCK AND ROLL HALL OF FAME

Leaders Can Cry...and Sometimes They Must

As newborn babies, we cry for everything, because it's the only vocalization we can manage. As we grow and develop, our ability to vocalize our needs and wants expands exponentially, but for some reason, the reality that humans cry often seems to get pushed to the side. We may not cry because we need to be fed anymore, but we still can cry for countless reasons: happiness, sadness, grief, anger, frustration, catharsis.

There is nothing wrong with a Leader shedding tears if the occasion calls for it. I have been to many first responder funerals (more than I wish) where tears were the order of the day. Many first responders feel that showing emotion equates to weakness. But if we can't show emotion at the death of a colleague, the death of a friend, the death of a family member, or even the death of someone you don't know, then what have we become?

It took me a long time, but I came to realize that there is nothing wrong with tears. For many years I was worried: people close to me died or were close to death, and I shed no tears. I thought that my job had made me cold, that I was closed off to this aspect of emotion.

Then PTS really dug its hooks into me, and I found myself crying at songs, commercials, movies.... I felt like I was on an emotional roller coaster half the time.

Once I started therapy for my trauma the truth became evident. Tears are a natural response to an incident that moves us. Humans have been crying for millennia. Leaders are human. Therefore, its ok for Leaders to cry when appropriate.

I wouldn't suggest melting down every time there is a crisis, as that is extremely exhausting, and not at all reassuring. But tears, when called for, show that you care, that you empathize, and that you are not afraid to show some vulnerability.

One striking example of this that always comes to mind for me is the reaction of President Barack Obama during his press conference after the Sandy Hook Elementary School shooting in December 2012. During his remarks, with the eyes of the world upon him, and with no shame, he stopped twice to compose himself and wipe away visible tears. The emotion, the magnitude of the event was clear on his face, but he knew that he was still expected to respond, and he did so masterfully. He didn't attempt to hide or downplay his emotional reaction, he left it on display for the world to see and spoke for a nation that was in mourning.

If tears are okay for the leader of the free world, then tears are okay for any Leader.

> **"Tears are the silent language of grief."**
> -VOLTAIRE, 17ᵀᴴ CENTURY FRENCH PHILOSOPHER,
> WRITER, AND RELIGIOUS ACTIVIST

"There is a sacredness in tears. They are not the mark of weakness, but of power. They speak more eloquently than ten thousand tongues. They are the messengers of overwhelming grief, of deep contrition, and of unspeakable love."

-WASHINGTON IRVING, AMERICAN SHORT STORY AUTHOR, BIOGRAPHER, ESSAYIST, AND DIPLOMAT

Have Difficult Conversations in a Timely Fashion

Leadership sometimes means having very difficult conversations. You can't be afraid to be honest about the big issues, even if you know it will hurt someone to hear the truth.

My psychologist did this for me when it came to my PTS diagnosis. She told me, very bluntly, that I had a serious mental health issue and that it would take work to get back to the father, the husband, the cop, and the man that I had been. Hearing this information laid out so quickly and cleanly was devastating to me, but her performance as a Leader; her honesty and willingness to be cruel to be kind, also left me with hope.

The core of these conversations is active listening. This is a skill that, as a Leader, you should endeavor to master. The easiest definition of active listening is this: seek to understand the person you're speaking with before you are understood. If you're struggling with that concept a bit, that's excellent, as it means that you're giving it some serious thought.

As someone who has had many of these difficult conversations sitting on both sides of the table, quite often about complex and sensitive personal issues, I learned very quickly when someone was hearing, but not listening. This is a horrible trait for someone who is privileged to be receiving this kind of sensitive, personal, life-altering information from the people they lead.

I recall one time when I was reporting the results of a statistical study I had done for my supervisor at the time. It was nothing overly complex, and I certainly didn't have any emotional investment in the report, but it did represent half a day of work. After a couple minutes it became apparent he didn't care, his eyes started drifting around, and at about the nine-minute mark he looked at me and said 'Listen, I'll be honest. This doesn't really concern me at all, so I haven't been listening." Incredulous, I put the papers down and asked if I could speak my mind freely, which he agreed to let me do. I told him, in no uncertain terms, that he had just committed one of the cardinal sins of leadership of any type, and that if I were a more junior officer, had been through fewer ups and downs in my career, or if I were still deep in the questioning of self-worth that PTS can cause, that he would have just lost any loyalty or respect he had earned from me. I don't know if he took my advice to heart or not, but at least I could never say that I hadn't done my best to speak my mind and educate him.

Rank or position does not a Leader make.

These tricky talks are potentially some of the most difficult tasks you will have as a Leader – these conversations can be emotional and psychological mine fields where you will have to ask some probing questions that the person you're speaking with may not want to rise to. These could include queries about mental health, work attendance, family situations, financial issues, or physical ailments. However, as a Leader you lose the luxury of avoiding these difficult discussions. (Think back to **Know Your Team** from earlier.) You owe it to those you lead to make sure that their health, well-being, and fit as part of your team is paramount, and that they know this.

Having these talks is both science and art. There's no set way to conduct them but being an active listener and showing genuine concern and empathy are very good starting points.

> "I don't need a friend who changes when I change and nods when I nod; my shadow does that much better."
>
> -PLUTARCH, 1ST CENTURY GREEK (WITH ROMAN CITIZENSHIP) PHILOSOPHER AND WRITER; FOLLOWER OF PLATO

> "Sometimes the most important conversations are the most difficult to engage in."
>
> -JEANNE PHILLIPS, AMERICAN AUTHOR; NEWSPAPER COLUMNIST OF 'DEAR ABBY'

If Someone Needs to Talk to You, Let Them Talk

When someone comes to you to talk, let them. As we just discussed, when you listen, practice active listening. This is a basic tenet of leadership, but quite often Leaders who have information or counsel they are anxious to offer will be champing at the bit to do so. After all, Leaders are helpers! Let the person talk, then, when the time is right, **and if you're asked**, offer your input. When someone is baring their soul to you, perhaps about something that has impacted them to their core; it's not the time to unload.

Many motivational speakers and leadership gurus call this 'power listening' or something similar. I can't think of a better way to describe it.

Years before my PTS was confirmed, I was having a conversation with a supervisor who, unfortunately, was firmly on the 'manager' end of the leadership scale. On one very bad day, I was trying to tell him that I thought something was wrong. Instead of listening, which was all I needed, he said something to the effect of "Yeah, that sucks," then launched into his own story about a collision he had been involved in when he was a rookie. I know everyone has their tale to tell, but at that moment I just wanted to feel like I was being heard and understood. Sometimes that's all it takes.

I do, however, now think about that officer (who ended his relationship with me on very negative terms) and wonder if he ever had his own opportunity to talk while someone simply listened. I've made a couple attempts to re-connect with this officer and have been rebuffed both times. I can only hope he's found a Leader for himself. Even more, I hope he's become a Leader himself.

> "We have two ears and one tongue so that we would listen more and talk less."
> -DIOGENES, 4TH CENTURY BC GREEK PHILOSOPHER; ONE OF THE FOUNDERS OF CYNIC PHILOSOPHY.

> "When people talk, listen completely. Most people never listen."
> -ERNEST HEMINGWAY, AMERICAN SHORT STORY AUTHOR, NOVELIST, JOURNALIST, AND NOBEL PRIZE WINNER

Grief Is a Path That Is Walked Alone...But You Can Help

As a Leader, it is inevitable that at some point you are either going to deal with grief – your own or someone else's.

Grief is a powerful, yet important emotion that allows for many things, dependent on the situation – saying goodbye; closure; remembrance; connection with family and friends; mourning; and, finally, moving on. Although most often thought of in terms of losing someone (death or relationship breakdown,) it can touch almost every area of your life.

As painful as it can be, grief is a necessary part of recovering from a crisis or tragedy. And it happens more often than you might think. When I think about my own life since 2012, when I was finally able to put a name to my PTS, I've coped with grief over multiple things:

-the state of my marriage and how I had treated Cathy and my sons.

-the years of chaos and isolation and pain I lost between Mike's death and starting recovery.

-the loss of a prestigious position that my career path had been building to for years.

-the death of my best friend, and the emotional loss of another (neither of which I ever grieved until long after the fact.)

-the destruction of friendships I caused through my selfish, arrogant actions.

-Mike's death itself (which I also didn't grieve until long after it happened.)

-the deaths of my grandfather (2005), grandmother (2015), father-in-law (2016), father (2017) and the near-death of my mother after a heart attack and multiple strokes (about two months after my dad died.)

I'm still not sure if I've grieved all these things properly, to be honest. I know that my reaction to crises has been molded by my career; my usual course of action during a crisis is to cope by taking charge of it as much as possible. I'm comfortable in that role and focusing on tasks and details is therapeutic for me. I have also been lucky in that during most of the times I listed, I had Leaders step up and offer me support and guidance. Sometimes it was simply a phone call, sometimes a classy gesture like arranging for a police presence and escort of my grandfather's funeral procession (he was what would now be called a Border Services Agent, but in his time, he simply 'worked for Customs.' He was my first role model for law enforcement.)

Coping with grief over the deeper issues of my marriage and career was an integral part of my therapy. My doctor worked with me through these issues, teaching me that until I could properly lay some of these demons to rest, I would never be able to move forward. One by one, we did so, and I can now look back and say that I feel I've closed the door properly on those parts of my PTS experience.

When you are faced with grief, whichever side of the desk you may be on, here are some suggestions to help smooth the way:

-realize that grief is a necessary part of the recovery process.

-communication between yourself and other people who are grieving the same thing creates connections and support.

-practice acceptance of small pieces of chaos in your everyday life so when things really go off the rails you have resiliency built up.

-don't isolate yourself and don't grieve in solitude.

-ask for help and support (this will be a recurring theme throughout this book;).

-if you are offering someone support, give them a safe space to do so.

How you handle grief can create a profound difference between bringing your life, or that of someone on your team, to a screeching, chaotic halt and creating an experience that allows for growth, reflection, remembrance, and possibly even laughter.

"Give sorrow words; the grief that does not speak knits up the o'er wrought heart and bids it break."
-William Shakespeare, Macbeth, Act 1V, Scene III

"Grief is the price we pay for love."
-Elizabeth II, Queen of England, and Head of the British Commonwealth since 1952, who lost her husband and consort Prince Philip in April 2021

Realize That You Can't Go It Alone

A huge part of Leadership includes recognizing when you can't do it all yourself. You will seldom find a true Leader who says that they reached the position they have on their own. They will talk about their mentors and teachers; leaders who both formed them AND provided them with really good bad examples.

It took me years to realize this, and countless times I hurt those around me through my ego, arrogance, and assumptions that I could defeat any problem on my own. In the last nine years, I have had countless Leaders in my life, both in uniform and out, who contributed to helping me regain my strength, my confidence, my empathy, my balance, my career, my marriage, and my health. It took me opening the door to those Leaders before I finally began to heal.

"I am not afraid of an army of lions led by a sheep; I am afraid of an army of sheep led by a lion."
 -ALEXANDER THE GREAT, 3ʳᵈ CENTURY BC KING OF MACEDONIA; CREATED ONE OF THE LARGEST EMPIRES OF THE ANCIENT WORLD BY THE AGE OF THIRTY, STRETCHING FROM GREECE TO NORTHWESTERN INDIA; UNDEFEATED IN BATTLE; WIDELY CONSIDERED ONE OF HISTORY'S MOST SUCCESSFUL MILITARY COMMANDERS

"No man will make a great leader who wants to do it all himself, or to get all the credit for doing it."
 -ANDREW CARNEGIE, SCOTTISH-AMERICAN INDUSTRIALIST, BUSINESS TYCOON, AND PHILANTHROPIST

You Need to Set the Example to Get the Buy-In

Lead by example, even if doing so is uncomfortable or you don't agree with the company line. If you do so, you'll get buy-in from those you lead and who will ultimately be responsible for the boots on the ground response to whatever new policy, initiative, or program is being implemented.

Here's a perfect example. In the last few years, mental health programming in Canada has made considerable progress. In the emergency response field, however, this hasn't always been met with the level of support from leaders that it should be. I have found that the true Leaders, even if they privately had doubts about a program or initiative, championed the effort, led the way through the training or policy change, and consistently encouraged their people to give the 'new stuff' a try.

Due to years of being so submerged in PTS information, I sometimes felt like I didn't really draw anything new from some of the training sessions I've been to. But I kept my reservations to myself, supported all the programming I could, and was thankful that our members were now getting at least the basic training they needed to start recognizing mental health issues in our brothers and sisters.

> "A leader is a dealer in hope."
> -NAPOLEON BONAPARTE, FRENCH STATESMAN AND MILITARY LEADER; LED SEVERAL SUCCESSFUL CAMPAIGNS DURING THE FRENCH REVOLUTIONARY WARS; EMPEROR OF FRANCE FROM 1804 UNTIL 1815

> "People buy into the leader before they buy into the vision."
> -JOHN C MAXWELL, AMERICAN MOTIVATIONAL SPEAKER, PASTOR, AND AUTHOR OF "21 IRREFUTABLE LAWS OF LEADERSHIP" AND "21 INDISPENSABLE QUALITIES OF A LEADER"

As a Leader, You Lose the Right to Have an Unpleasant Day

As a Leader, you set the tone around the office, the shop, the lab, the station, the store, the rink, the battlefield, or wherever it is you Lead.

I remember a discussion I had a few years ago with a leader (who had the ability to become a Capital-L Leader, if she had really wanted to,) who walked into our office, ignored the good morning greetings from her shift, and slammed the door of the supervisor's office. I would later find out that she had a nasty argument with her spouse before coming to work that morning, but before I found that out I watched those officers, who were coming in from their stretch of five days off fresh and ready to take on the world, deflate before my eyes as the person who they expected to Lead them drained away their enthusiasm and sent them shuffling out the door to their day's work.

When you are a Leader, all eyes are on you. Your mood, your energy, your enthusiasm; these are the things that your people are watching (and hoping) for to kick off your time together. Conversely, if you demonstrate none of these things, your team will absorb that just as readily and they will shut down before your day even really begins.

I recognized so much of myself in that moment and was able to turn that slammed door into a powerful, teachable moment during a conversation with her about the value of leaving your difficult day at the door and how important it was to be the thing you wanted those who follow you to be.

If you are upset, your team will know it. When you are frustrated, emotions can often overpower your logic. Better to tell your people that you need to step away from the scene for a few minutes, compose yourself, get your emotions under control, and then re-engage with your troops.

> "I cannot trust a man to control others who cannot control himself."
>
> -ROBERT E LEE, AMERICAN AND CONFEDERATE SOLDIER; COMMANDER OF THE CONFEDERATE STATES ARMY IN THE AMERICAN CIVIL WAR FROM 1862 UNTIL HIS SURRENDER IN 1865

> "An employee's motivation is a direct result of the sum of interactions with his or her manager."
>
> -DR. BOB NELSON, AMERICAN MOTIVATIONAL SPEAKER, AND AUTHOR OF "KEEPING UP IN A DOWN ECONOMY", "1001 WAYS TO ENERGIZE EMPLOYEES", AND "MANAGING FOR DUMMIES" AMONG MANY OTHERS

Anger Quite Often Isn't Anger

Anger is perhaps the strongest emotion. It manifests itself quickly and can lead to extremely violent and aggressive interactions. During my twenty years of policing, I've witnessed, been subjected to, and defused anger thousands of times.

The thing is, quite often anger is not really anger. It is an easy catch-all for many other emotions: shame, guilt, sadness, grief, fear, remorse, abandonment, isolation. 'Anger' is simply easier to put a name to.

As a Leader, you will often be confronted with 'anger.' One of the keys to conflict resolution is peeling back the layers to find out what the real emotion you're dealing with is.

This doesn't have to be a complex process; in fact, the easier you can make it, the better. During some very hostile conversations I've had in the past few years, I've found it easiest to stick to a simple template:

A – try to get the person you're speaking with to use "I" statements that provide clarification (knowledge is power!).

B – use statements about how you feel as the Leader who has the ear of the person who is upset.

C – stay in the here and now (this is particularly important when you are speaking to someone who may be dealing with trauma.)

A dialogue following this template might play out like so:

Leader: "I asked you to come sit down because it seems like you're not really yourself today. What's going on?" (Know your people!)

Listener: "I'm still mad about getting written up last week. It's unfair. It's complete BS."

Leader: "OK, that's fair. I'm wondering, though. Are you upset at getting written up, even though you admitted that you didn't follow the proper procedure? Or is there something else? Do you feel like you've never been trained properly on what you should have done? Or are you feeling targeted because other people have done the same thing with different results? Can you try and expand a bit for me? I feel like there's more going on here and I want you to walk out of my office with a resolution and feeling better about how this all went down."

Listener: (after some thought.) "I think that's it. I'm angry because no one ever really showed me how to fill out that paperwork. You guys do it differently here than at the last office I worked at and when I sat down to do the paperwork, everyone just took off."

Leader: "I can understand why that would bug you. So, it feels to me like you're more disappointed or feeling let down by your shift and your supervisor. But since you haven't had a chance to tell anyone that, it just looks to everyone like you're angry at the world."

Listener: "That's a good word, disappointed. And when I tried to explain, everyone just kept saying 'It's informal, it's not a big deal.' But I've never had any kind of documentation laid on me before and it's really bugging me. I'm also mad at myself because I've had chances to ask how to do those reports and never did anything about it. So, I guess I'm not really angry at the discipline thing."

Leader: "Ok, this all makes a lot more sense now. Listen, these things can be overcome. Why don't we run over the policy now and I can walk you through the paperwork? I won't overrule what your supervisor did, but I'm willing to have a chat with them about this whole thing and maybe there's something we can do about the informal."

Listener: "I'd appreciate that. Thanks. I'm feeling way better about this."

Leader: "My door is always open."

Of course, not every chat goes this smoothly – in the first responder world, they often involve a lot more swearing – but if you can keep to this kind of simple back and forth, this template is applicable to almost any situation.

Actually, it can be applied to almost any conflict in general. Consider how easy it would be to apply these to an argument with your spouse or kids. "I'm angry because…" and 'I feel X because…" are excellent open-ended tools for starting and sustaining a productive back and forth dialogue.

In 2012, when I was in the depths of starting to fix both myself and our marriage, Cathy and I had many, many of these kinds of talks, where we tried to be as productive as possible, even though the conversations were brimming with emotion that could easily boil over (and to be honest, sometimes did.) This has become our standard operating procedure for when we are tackling any heavy discussions, including with our kids.

'Anger' can be a very effective means to an end.

> **"Anybody can become angry — that is easy, but to be angry with the right person and to the right degree and at the right time and for the right purpose, and in the right way — that is not within everybody's power and is not easy."**
>
> -ARISTOTLE, GREEK PHILOSOPHER, SCIENTIST, AND POET

> **"Anger ventilated often hurries towards forgiveness; and concealed often hardens into revenge."**
>
> -LORD EDWARD BULWER-LYTTON, ENGLISH NOVELIST, POET, PLAYWRIGHT, AND POLITICIAN; ORIGINATOR OF THE LITERARY TERMS "THE GREAT UNWASHED", "PURSUIT OF THE ALMIGHTY DOLLAR", "THE PEN IS MIGHTIER THAN THE SWORD", "DWELLER ON THE THRESHOLD", AND THE CLASSIC OPENING LINE "IT WAS A DARK AND STORMY NIGHT"

Make Sure Your Open Door Is Really Open and Not Just Lip Service

Many leaders claim to have an 'open door policy'. If, as a Leader, you say that your door is always open, make sure it truly is. Having that open door means that you are willing to put aside your phone calls, your computer, your texts, and the things on your agenda to listen to someone on what might turn out to be the worst day of their life. Your words could be someone's lifeline.

I've been on both sides of that conversation: I'm thinking back to telling that very first Leader who listened to me about my PTS and the problems I was having in my marriage at the same time. But I'm also thinking of my own lifelong stance that

Leaders should have an open door and, because I believe that, being told stories of domestic abuse, miscarried children, substance abuse issues, impending divorces, and life-altering health issues.

In all honesty, it may not always be a suitable time to talk, and if you are amid something critical you owe it to your people to tell them that. There is nothing worse than someone who is hoping for a sympathetic ear and a shoulder to cry on to see the person they are counting on checking their phone or scanning their computer screen.

However, this is where knowing your people comes into play. On even the busiest day, if you recognize that someone you Lead is truly in crisis, you may have to close your laptop, clear your schedule, take your phone off the hook, and become the Leader that person needs at that moment. Those instances of someone coming to you so you can be their pillar of strength are one of the highest honors a Leader can have.

> "Words are, of course, the most powerful drug used by mankind."
>
> -RUDYARD KIPLING, ENGLISH JOURNALIST, SHORT-STORY WRITER, POET, AND NOVELIST

> "A true leader has to have a genuine open-door policy so that his people are not afraid to approach him for any reason."
>
> -HAROLD S GENEEN, AMERICAN BUSINESS MAGNATE; PRESIDENT OF ITT CORPORATION; CO-AUTHOR OF 4 NY TIMES BEST-SELLING BUSINESS MANAGEMENT BOOKS

Pick the Hill You Want to Die On

If your definition of 'hero' is someone who must take on the difficulties of the world themselves, then you should also remember the corollary to this: heroes often die alone.

> "Show me a hero, and I'll write you a tragedy."
> -F Scott Fitzgerald, American writer whose works helped define the 'Jazz Age'

> "There's a thin line between being a hero and being a memory."
> -Optimus Prime, Autobot leader; Transformer; transport truck; surprisingly relevant leadership role model of the author

Get in Front of Mistakes, Admit Them, and Control the Damage

Leaders with foresight and who have a grasp of the big picture get in front of issues and do their damndest to minimize the damage, even while admitting to the damage already done.

In 2012, the Ombudsman of Ontario (the province in Canada where I live) released a scathing report that heavily criticized how police services were handling PTS and other operational stress injuries. The day the report was released; (in fact, within an hour or so of the report becoming public), a Leader high-up in my organization distributed the document to area commanders, openly admitted that our organization had taken a pounding in the report and urged us to make discussion of the issue with our people a priority.

There was no attempt at whitewashing, no wordsmithing – we fared poorly as an organization and this Leader pulled no punches in telling us that. That Leader's honesty and integrity, in turn, inspired me to do more than simply share the weblink to the report and ask the 150 or so people I was responsible for at that time to read it; it inspired me to send the email telling my story as I discussed previously. That decision led to those ten seconds of terror I alluded to earlier when I was talking about living out loud. But those ten seconds of terror have led to a lifetime's worth of growth in just under a decade.

Isn't it funny how these traits of Leadership keep circling back on themselves?

> **"No one should be ashamed to admit they are wrong, which is but saying, in other words, that they are wiser today than they were yesterday."**
> -ALEXANDER POPE, ENGLISH POET; BEST KNOWN FOR HIS SATIRICAL VERSE, HIS TRANSLATION OF HOMER AND FOR HIS USE OF THE HEROIC COUPLET

> **"It is the highest form of self-respect to admit our errors and mistakes and make amends for them. To make a mistake is only an error in judgment, but to adhere to it when it is discovered shows infirmity of character."**
> -DALE E TURNER, AMERICAN ACTOR, SCREENWRITER, PRODUCER, AND MOTIVATIONAL SPEAKER

Your Role in a Crisis

As a Leader, in a crisis, you have a few critical tasks:

1 – Say something about the crisis.
2 – Make decisions about the crisis.

Silence can be an effective tool for a Leader, in the right circumstances, but it takes a master to know how to use it properly. Silence during a crisis is not one of those circumstances. Your people need to hear from you in a critical situation. They need to know that you recognize a crisis, that you are stepping up to take charge, and that you are going to make decisions. Then they need to see you make those decisions. There is nothing more disheartening than an indecisive Leader.

Even if the decision you make is ultimately wrong, if you made it based on the information you had at hand, to the best of your knowledge, skills, and abilities, then you have done what you can as a Leader.

And that's not to say that you must make all those decisions completely on your own. Remember that saying about heroes dying alone? A crisis is not the time to do so. Reach out to your people, your experts, your thinkers as well as your doers, regardless of where they sit in the line of seniority above or below you.

As I write this, I'm recalling several times when first responders I knew killed themselves. Although it was never definitively proven that any or all of them were dealing with PTS, the popular consensus is that they were. The reactions by leadership to these different deaths, which took place across different emergency response disciplines and organizations, were fascinating to watch unfold.

In some of the cases, little to no information was given to the deceased's co-workers, leaving them to fill in gaps themselves, and frustrated at feeling they could not properly mourn their peer and partner.

In two specific others I can think of, one of which I was present for, the senior officer assigned to deal with the death organized briefings for all who wanted to attend, confirmed that the individual had killed themselves, shared the information that the family was comfortable sharing, and then ended the session with reminding all in attendance of the mental health supports available and providing written materials about those supports. In both cases, the briefing officer was clearly moved and feeling emotional at the circumstances yet maintained their professionalism and provided light at a very dark time.

They were both Capital-L Leaders in their words, actions, and attitudes. Their responses were textbook examples of what those you have the privilege to lead need from you when uncertainty is ruling the day.

The skills involved with conducting after-action debriefings (or whatever your profession calls them) can be honed through training and practice. These quick sit-downs, if done soon after a critical incident, can be extremely beneficial both in reducing the impact the critical incident may have and increasing the resiliency with which your team can begin to recover. The keys are simple:

-acknowledge that an incident has occurred and that it may have an impact.

-inform your troops of what they can expect and of what resources are available.

-respond to any questions or concerns your team has.

REMEMBER – either you or someone on your team may not have any reaction at all when others seem to be much more impacted. That's fine. As I've said, trauma is relative – your reaction is your reaction, and no one can claim that what you feel is 'wrong.'

If you're not comfortable leading these kinds of debriefings, most employers (and pretty much all first responder agencies at this point) have access to critical incident stress response teams either internally or contracted out. The people on these teams are experts in bringing a group together, easing any skepticism, bringing their concerns and fears out, and leaving everyone feeling empowered and prepared for what might lie ahead. They are worth their weight in gold.

In fact, critical incidents can provide excellent opportunities for self-reflection with regards to your own reactions and responses. I wouldn't suggest attempting to digest things while you're in crisis mode, but when you get some quiet time to reflect, it's well worth your time to do so.

> "In any moment of decision, the best thing you can do is the right thing, the next best thing is the wrong thing, and the worst thing you can do is nothing."
>
> -THEODORE ROOSEVELT, 26TH PRESIDENT OF THE UNITED STATES, AUTHOR, EXPLORER, SOLDIER, NATURALIST

"In crisis management, be quick with the facts, slow with the blame."

-Leonard Saffir, Executive VP of Porter Novelli, one of largest public relations firms in the world; author of multiple best-selling crisis management textbooks

Know When to Talk and When to Act

There's a time for talk, and a time for action. Capital-L Leadership is recognizing which is which.

I'm writing this relating to the earlier piece about having an open-door policy. If you recognize one of your people is in crisis, act, don't simply talk about it. No one wants to hear that someone they respect agrees that they are in a state of crisis, and then be given platitudes about how "it will be okay" or how "you'll get through this." There should never be a 'you' when it comes to getting through a tough time, there should only be 'we.'

The actions you could take are myriad – keep talking them through the problem, connect them with your internal peer support system, take them off-duty and make sure they get home safely, connect with their spouse or family, even get them to medical attention if needed. These are incidents of situational

Leadership, and your response will, by necessity, be different every time.

There is, of course, the possibility that the person coming to you will not necessarily want help. They may simply want to unload something and get it off their chest. I have been told many times "But please don't tell anyone!" after someone tells their tale. As a Leader, this is an awkward, uncomfortable position to be in. If you sense the discussion going this way, make sure that you use your discretion, set boundaries, and ensure that the person you're speaking with is aware of those boundaries with regards to legal, ethical, and professional obligations that you both may have.

One strong suggestion to keep in mind. One thing that should never, ever be offered to someone in crisis is pity. No one who is in a helping profession ever wants to be pitied. And for good reason – it's ultimately a hollow emotion that benefits neither party. Show empathy, not pity, and you will absolutely get a much better reaction and better buy-in.

> **"The proof of battle is action, the proof of words, debate. No time for speeches now, it's time to fight."**
> -HOMER, 8TH CENTURY BC GREEK AUTHOR OF THE ILIAD AND THE ODYSSEY, EPIC POEMS WHICH FORM THE BASIS FOR ALMOST ALL GREEK LITERATURE

> **"Action expresses priorities."**
> -MAHATMA MOHANDAS GANDHI, INDIAN ACTIVIST AGAINST BRITISH COLONIAL RULE AND PROPONENT OF NON-VIOLENT CIVIL DISOBEDIENCE

'Career Suicide' is Overrated

Sometimes, an action that is termed 'career suicide' (by people who you would think know what that looks like,) can have the greatest impact on the most people. 'Career suicide', or the prospect of it, is a very real possibility when you live out loud as a Leader.

When I sent my PTS story out to my peers in 2012, within a few hours it had gone 'viral', at least in the policing world, and by the next morning I was getting comments and acknowledgments of my tale from officers throughout my police service, and beyond. Because of this email, I had three officers higher in rank tell me, in separate conversations, that I had committed 'career suicide' and that making this disclosure would come back to haunt me when I sought future opportunities or promotions. My reply to that was, paraphrased, that if such an act was career suicide, then perhaps I had hit my limit of rank and would be happy to stay where I was.

As it turned out, it wasn't career suicide at all.

Since sending that email nine years ago, I've been offered opportunities and had experiences that I never would have had otherwise. I came to realize that, whereas years ago I felt I *had* to climb that ladder, *had* to achieve promotions; now I can enjoy the pace of my career and pick and choose how and when I move (which I finally did, in September of 2018, returning to the rank of Staff Sergeant.)

I will never regret my act of 'career suicide!

"Be the flame, not the moth."

-GIACOMO CASANOVA, 18TH CENTURY ITALIAN ADVENTURER AND AUTHOR; SO FAMOUS FOR HIS OFTEN COMPLICATED AND ELABORATE RELATIONSHIPS WITH WOMEN THAT HIS NAME IS NOW SYNONYMOUS WITH "WOMANIZER"

"Your profession is not what brings home your weekly paycheck, your profession is what you're put here on earth to do, with such passion and such intensity that it becomes spiritual in calling."

-VINCENT VAN GOGH, PROLIFIC DUTCH POST-IMPRESSIONIST PAINTER

There Are Stars in Even the Darkest Sky...You May Just Have to Strain to See Them

When you're a Leader, you must believe that even the darkest times have bright spots and an end. It's easy to get overwhelmed when that darkness is settling in and remembering that there will eventually be a light at the end can provide an incredible boost to someone's spirit and resolve.

In the depths of my PTS, I had days when I could barely get out of bed; when I couldn't figure out what uniform shirt to grab out of the ten I had that were all the same; that I couldn't even imagine doing things like making doctor's appointments or filling out paperwork. During those days, Cathy is the one who kept reminding me over and over that these days wouldn't last forever. She's the one who gave me the kick in the ass that I needed when I couldn't figure out how to start my day. She was the Leader I needed; a Leader that I wasn't capable of being at that point.

As dark as those days were, they taught me a lesson – a Leader's role when things look their blackest is to pick out the diamonds in the coal, polish them, and put them on a pedestal to inspire both the Leader and those they lead.

> "There is no easy way from the earth to the stars."
>
> -SENECA, ROMAN WRITER, PHILOSOPHER, AND RHETORICIAN

> "It is often in the darkest skies that we see the brightest stars."
>
> -RICHARD EVANS, BRITISH HISTORIAN FOCUSING ON WORLD WAR II EUROPE; REGIUS PROFESSOR OF HISTORY AT CAMBRIDGE

Mistakes Exist Until You Acknowledge Them

Leaders are never afraid to admit that they've made a mistake, even one that was made in the past and may be long forgotten. When I first opened up about my PTS, and told my story, I received a touching email from a police officer who I consider to be THE Leader. He is the officer that, even now, over twenty years after first being led by him, most shapes my decision making when it comes to issues of leadership. He was my first platoon Sergeant when I started working for my current police service, then was my Staff Sergeant the first time I was ever an acting supervisor. I respect him more than anyone else I've ever met in my professional life.

But back to that email.

During the time I mentioned when I was getting responses almost hourly to the PTS story I had sent out via email, I opened a message from him. In that email, he apologized for missing the signs I talked about. He felt that, as my immediate supervisor, he should have seen that I had changed, that I was different and not myself. He then alluded to things in his own extensive career that had left a mark on him, apologized again for not reaching out at the time of Mike's death, and invited me for coffee.

I remember struggling with how to reply for several days. How does one start to acknowledge such a humbling and open sentiment? It had been almost a decade since Mike's collision, this Leader had climbed the rank structure to point where he now had an incredible amount of responsibility and obligation, and he hadn't 'missed' anything. I didn't show or tell anyone that I had been impacted by Mike's death, so unless someone was doing nothing but watching me constantly, they never would have picked up the subtle changes I was undergoing. How could he have missed what wasn't really on display? Yet, here he was, apologizing to me for imagined errors and omissions. I thought at that point that this Leader had taught me all he could about leadership, yet here he was with something completely new from the playbook.

My reply ended up being simple. I thanked him for checking in with me and for still looking out for me. I assured him that he hadn't missed anything all those years ago; in fact, the stability and consistency that came from working with him were one of the touchstones that helped during the early days of riding out this storm back in 2004. I assured him that I still thought the same of him as I did back then and thanked him for providing me with yet another lesson in what it meant to truly be a Leader. We've had some very enjoyable chats over coffee since then and I continue to be grateful that I have a role model of his caliber to continue learning from.

Always take the opportunity to sit at the feet of a master.

"Mistakes are portals of discovery."

-JAMES JOYCE, IRISH NOVELIST, SHORT STORY WRITER, AND POET; MODERNIST AVANT-GARDE WRITER; REGARDED AS ONE OF THE MOST INFLUENTIAL AUTHORS OF THE 20TH CENTURY

"Mistakes are always forgivable, if one has the courage to admit them."

-BRUCE LEE, LEGENDARY HONG KONG / AMERICAN ACTOR, DIRECTOR, MARTIAL ARTIST, TEACHER, AND PHILOSOPHER; FOUNDER OF JEET KUNE DO

No Leader Is an Island

True Leaders thrive on being surrounded by other Leaders. Or, even better, people aspiring to be Leaders who are willing to take risks, make mistakes, and live out loud. Great feats are seldom accomplished by oneself.

If you can't learn that lesson, then learn the corollary - even the biggest islands can be flooded when the storm is bad enough. For a few years, I was an island which was swamped over and over, for that exact reason – I thought I could do it all myself.

Eventually, you get tired of being cold and soaked and you learn that you need other people to help pull you from the water.

"No man is an island, entire of itself; every man is a piece of the continent, a part of the main…And therefore never send to know for whom the bell tolls, it tolls for thee."

-JOHN DONNE, ENGLISH POET, AND CLERIC IN THE CHURCH OF ENGLAND; CONSIDERED THE PRE-EMINENT REPRESENTATIVE OF THE METAPHYSICAL RENAISSANCE POETS

"Before you are a leader, success is all about growing yourself. When you become a leader, success is all about growing others."

-JACK WELCH, RETIRED CHAIRMAN AND CEO OF GENERAL ELECTRIC, AUTHOR, AND FOUNDER OF THE JACK WELCH MANAGEMENT INSTITUTE

Perception Is Not Reality

You never know what's going on in someone else's life and what may be causing them to be in crisis. The answer to this is simple. Don't let your perceptions rule your actions. Don't guess, don't assume, and don't judge – verify appearances with facts by **asking the person!**

I made this mistake several years ago with a manager who I was attempting to tell about my traumatic incident. I was soundly rebuffed, and this leader clearly didn't want to discuss the issue. For years, I was angry at that leader for the way he reacted, for not giving me a chance to share.

Looking back now, I'm reasonably sure this officer was dealing with his own issues. Instead of looking at this interaction as an opportunity to give the officer a chance to tell his own story, I assumed that he was just being a jerk and ended the conversation. If I had the chance to do it again, I would have asked this officer if he had something that he wanted to get off his chest and make a sincere, earnest effort to get him to open up. Instead,

I made assumptions and judgments and ultimately lost out not only on a chance to share my own burden, but to let a fellow officer do the same.

> "Perception is strong and sight weak. In strategy it is important to see distant things as if they were close and to take a distanced view of close things."
> -MIYAMOTO MUSASHI, 16TH CENTURY JAPANESE SWORDSMAN, MARTIAL ARTIST, PHILOSOPHER, AND *RONIN* (A ROGUE SAMURAI WITH NO MASTER)

> "What you see and hear depends a good deal on where you are standing; it also depends on what sort of person you are."
> -CS LEWIS, BRITISH NOVELIST, POET, ACADEMIC, LITERARY CRITIC, ESSAYIST, BROADCASTER, LECTURER

Follow Your Own Counsel and Look in the Mirror

Sometimes, the best leadership lessons come from looking in the mirror and taking your own advice. This is a concept that I missed for almost five years.

During those years, I was part of my police service's internal peer support team. My role during that time was to assist officers who had been through a critical incident, leading debriefings with either groups or individual officers. Dozens of times, I sat and expounded on the signs and symptoms that these officers should be looking for in themselves in the days following the incidents they had been part of. Not once during those years did I ever look in the mirror, either literally or figuratively, and realize that these signs of PTS were my day-to-day reality.

When I was in the grip of my growing PTS, I never took any serious time to reflect about anything. Marriage, fatherhood, career; I was simply bouncing from one crisis to the next, assuming that things would get taken care of at home and only knowing that I wanted more and more promotions and responsibility at work. I never gave myself quiet moments to simply sit and look at the state of my life.

Good Leaders should do this frequently, gauging the temperature and pulse of their organizations and those they lead as well as themselves. If I had taken time to do this, it's very likely that I would have noticed that things were spinning madly around me and taken steps to stop the spin long before I finally crashed at the end of my long downwards spiral.

Capital-L Leaders are naturally given to self-reflection and self-discovery. These are how Leaders grow. If you're not currently engaging in these practices, I urge you to start. What you find out about yourself after careful and deliberate thought can be incredibly beneficial and lead to massive growth.

However, be prepared – this kind of introspection can be very painful. If you're honest with yourself, you will not only consider your accomplishments, but your non-successes (I hate the word failure!) as well. To do otherwise is to do yourself a disservice as a Leader.

This reflection must be measured, however. It is very easy to 'what if' and 'if only' yourself into inaction. Mistakes are a natural part of Leadership; the key is to learn from them, not constantly revisit and dissect them *ad infinitum*.

This was one of the lessons I had to learn about the night of Mike's death. I spent years reliving what I felt I had done wrong that night, things I felt had contributed to Mike's death. Things that I felt made me a failure. Those 'mistakes' weren't really mistakes – it simply took me a long time to realize that. Time, and a doctor who kindly reviewed Mike's injuries and death and assured me that there was nothing I could have done.

Only then did I realize that I had done my best with the training and equipment I had at my disposal. There is no shame in that.

Constant second guessing of yourself leads to self-doubt and shakes your self-confidence, which are two traits that a Leader needs to feel are unflappable even at the worst of times.

Within the last few years, I've taken part in several Mastermind groups. A couple of them have included other first responders, some of whom were also grappling with trauma. In looking back, it is extremely heartening to see the level of deep soul-searching that we have been able to undertake together, running the gamut of emotions from sadness to guilt to rage to grief to joy. I've learned more about myself through these groups than through any leadership or management training program I've ever taken. If you've never explored the Mastermind concept, do yourself and your Leadership skills a favor and see if you can involve yourself in a group, either online or in the real world.

Leaders always embrace the opportunity to grow and learn – the desire to better yourself should always be part of your drive as a Leader.

> **"Any man can make mistakes, but only an idiot persists in his error."**
>
> -CICERO, 1ST CENTURY BC ROMAN POLITICIAN AND LAWYER; ROMAN CONSUL IN 63 BC, CONSIDERED ONE OF ROMAN HISTORY'S GREATEST SPEAKERS; PRIMARY INFLUENCER OF WESTERN CIVILIZATION'S WRITING STYLE

> **"I learn from my mistakes. It's a very painful way to learn, but without pain, the old saying is, there's no gain."**
>
> -JOHNNY CASH, AMERICAN SINGER, SONGWRITER, ACTOR, AND AUTHOR

Leadership Is a Pilgrimage

The basis for this notation is a terribly cliched saying, but also a true one. Leaders make life about the journey, not the destination. They realize that every day is a potential gift, starting fresh with promise, which should be treasured, nurtured, and enjoyed to its fullest.

I didn't fully learn this lesson until the age of 40. My whole life, I pushed myself through everything I ever did – education, career, community service, relationships, everything. This meant that I had lots of accomplishments under my belt, many of which I achieved at a younger than usual age, but it also meant that I missed out on many of the simple, day-to-day rewards that life has to offer. I was a Staff Sergeant by the age of 35 and an Inspector by the age of 40. I would subsequently lose both of those ranks by choice – one unintended and one deliberate, but the fact remains that I achieved them. At times, I sought them to the exclusion of everything else.

I would later carry on this trait when it came to dealing with the increasingly impactful effects of poor decision making and trauma on my life. I substituted ambition and achievement for confronting these growing issues head on and dealing with the guilt, fear, anger, and doubt that had begun claiming my life.

I learned a very hard lesson on this – Leaders don't try to outrun their issues; they tackle them head on, no matter how unpleasant, and minimize the damage those issues can cause before they tear through everything around the Leader. To do otherwise is a disservice to those the Leader leads.

> "The mind is not a vessel to be filled, but a fire to be kindled."
>
> -Plutarch, 1st century Greek (with Roman citizenship) philosopher and writer; follower of Plato

> "If the path before you is clear, you're probably on somebody else's path."
>
> -Joseph Campbell, American author, mythologist, professor, and lecturer

Vulnerability Is Not a Weakness

Leaders let people see the demons they carry. None of us are perfect, and admitting flaws and mistakes not only shows the integrity of a Leader, but sets an example that it is acceptable, nay, necessary, to have admitted flaws.

The key is this: Leaders don't let those they lead see the demons overwhelming them. There is a substantial difference between showing your shortcomings and letting them run rampant. The best Leaders I have known have never been afraid to show that they aren't perfect but have also always been careful to manage the impact those issues may have on them.

It's perfectly acceptable to show emotion, to empathize with your troops, to laugh at a good joke (especially if it's at your expense,) even to cry when the situation dictates (see **Leaders Can Cry…and Sometimes They Must**.)

What isn't acceptable is to lose control or collapse. Losing control is a sign that your leadership isn't definite, and, depending on the situation, could literally mean life or death. If you control your own emotions, you help those around you control theirs.

> "Out of your vulnerabilities will come your strengths."
> —Sigmund Freud, Austrian neurologist; founder of psychoanalysis

> "Vulnerability is the only authentic state. Being vulnerable means being open, for wounding, but also for pleasure. Being open to the wounds of life means also being open to the bounty and beauty. Don't mask or deny your vulnerability: it is your greatest asset. Be vulnerable: quake and shake in your boots with it. the new goodness that is coming to you, in the form of people, situations, and things can only come to you when you are vulnerable."
> —Stephen Russell "The Barefoot Doctor", British teacher of Taoist philosophy, martial artist, and author

Trauma Doesn't Have to Be the End of Anything

Experiencing a trauma doesn't mean the end of your career, your marriage, parenting, your accomplishments, anything. Unless you let it. Mental health is not a one-way street, but a continuum; a sliding scale on which you will move from end to end your whole life.

When I was doing research for my first book, I interviewed several hundred first responders from across North America. Consistently, fear of losing their job was among the top causes of added stress. In fact, I have spoken to many uniform personnel from all different fields who have simply been cut loose when they told their employer they were dealing with an operational stress injury.

I'm not talking about the possibility of losing out on something like with my 'career suicide' example earlier, I'm talking about a full termination of their employment, sometimes effective immediately. On top of the medical and psychological issues the trauma is causing, there is now also financial stress due to job loss. It's little wonder that in many cases, first responders choose to keep their demons a complete secret – it's self-preservation.

When you're in the middle of a tornado, it can be very difficult to see this, but crises can present opportunities. Once your basic survival needs are taken care of, and you can step back to view the crisis with some perspective, you can start to see diamonds in the coal mine. Perhaps it's a change of role at work, a change of work location, even a change in career path.

This is admittedly, a very difficult topic to contemplate. With so many combinations of how employers and governments treat employees dealing with operational stress injuries, it's almost impossible to determine exactly how any one person's scenario will play out.

What I will say is this. Admitting that you are dealing with trauma, or another OSI, does not mean that you're not cut out for your uniform or your chosen path. That is defeatist thinking, and that mindset is what's led to decades of stigma that has irreparably damaged, even killed, countless first responders.

The thought that something that you've experienced because of performing the job you love has now rendered you unfit for that job seems ludicrous, yet here we are in 2021 with people from all walks still afraid to discuss the issue because they fear that they will be branded as unfit or broken.

You only break when you let the demons win.

"Only the dead have seen the end of war."
-PLATO, 4TH CENTURY GREEK PHILOSOPHER; STUDENT OF SOCRATES AND THE TEACHER OF ARISTOTLE; GENERALLY CONSIDERED ONE OF THE PIVOTAL THINKERS IN THE HISTORY OF PHILOSOPHY

> "I may not have gone where I intended to go, but I think I've ended up where I needed to be."
>
> -Douglas Adams, English author, scriptwriter, essayist, humorist, satirist, and dramatist; author of 'The Hitchhiker's Guide to the Galaxy' series

Hypocrisy Serves No One

Leaders cannot afford to be hypocritical. It is an extremely easy trap to fall into, that of 'do as I say, not as I do', especially when you have superior rank or position to those you lead.

If you are a leader who constantly puts themselves before those they lead, then expect to get bogged down in negativity, toxicity, and rumors. It is crucial that Leaders be individuals whose words and deeds match. As a Leader, you must recognize and eliminate hypocrisy when it rears its ugly head.

And it will.

I have a poster on my wall that I started using the day I was promoted into a Leadership position: "You are what you do, not what you say you'll do." (As much as I would love to take credit for this, it's a quote from the famous Swiss psychiatrist Carl Jung.)

I firmly believe this, and have tried to live that credo, even during the darkest days of my trauma: by living out loud, by talking about PTS and other OSIs, by giving officers the same kindness and support the most impactful Leaders had gave me.

Painfully, it must be admitted, also through reflecting on things I said I would do as a father, husband, and friend that I never did, or at least didn't do for a long time. Self-reflection can be a bitch.

Unfortunately, I have seen the opposite of this in many, many leaders when it comes to the area of trauma and its impact. *Corporately*, their organization has a plan in place to address OSIs, and *corporately* they acknowledge the tremendous damage it can do to both individuals and the organization, but in private they deride the programming, fail to support or implement it, and continue to adhere to outmoded ways of thinking about trauma. (See also **You Need to Set the Example to Get the Buy-In.**)

We're not discussing some guideline about meal claims or dry-cleaning allowances, we're talking about policies and programming that go to the very core of Leadership: taking care of your people when they need it. When it comes to that, there is no room for opinion about the tools that personnel have been given or have access to that would allow them to start seeking help for something that has affected them profoundly.

Make no mistake, as a Leader it will take soul-searching and reflection to recognize when you're being hypocritical, sometimes in the heat of a moment, sometimes over a longer term as an issue unfolds. But if you want to maintain your integrity, your perspective, and the trust of those you Lead, it is a critical skill to learn and practice.

> "One should examine oneself for a very long time before thinking of condemning others."
>
> -MOLIERE, FRENCH PLAYWRIGHT, AND ACTOR; CONSIDERED AMONG THE GREATEST WRITERS OF COMEDY IN WESTERN LITERATURE

> "No power can be maintained when it is only represented by hypocrites."
>
> -FRIEDRICH NIETZSCHE, GERMAN PHILOSOPHER, COMPOSER, POET, AND SCHOLAR

Communication – The Lifeblood of Leadership

As a Leader, a huge part of your role will involve communicating. Often, as previously alluded to, this will be difficult, not through any issue on your part, but because there are simply conversations that, due to their nature or content, are difficult to have.

Conversations never go the same way twice. This is because there are so many numerous factors to consider on both sides of the equation. Here's just a few:

Speaker – their words, their body language, their tone and cadence, their perceptions, their authority

Listener – their perceptions, their level of engagement, their pre-conceived outcome of the conversation

Not to mention, on both sides, the biases, history, culture, gender, mood, and psychological and physical state of the participants.

All is not lost, however. The building blocks of powerful conversations can be found in the 5 Ws (and one H):

-who do you talk to.
-what do you talk about.
-where do you talk.
-when do you talk.
-why do you talk.
-how do you talk.

During my journey through PTS, I've experienced hundreds of conversations on sensitive and personal topics with both uniformed and civilian personnel. I've also been on the other side of the desk, having to open to someone and discuss items around things like my psychological health and fitness for duty. Those conversations have given me some unique insight into the 5 Ws (and one H) of difficult conversations.

Who – as a Leader, you should be able to have a conversation, be it light and airy or serious and grounded, with anyone on your team. The definition of 'your team' is often flexible. In my world, for example, 'my team' could be a handful of civilian employees who work surrounded by police officers every day, a small platoon-sized groups of officers, a team of Sergeants, a detachment of fifty people, or, at a critical incident, a mixed team of regular officers and specialists. While you will of course have people, who are more comfortable with you than others, as a Leader you should make yourself equally available to everyone who you are hoping to make it through that day with. (One caveat – dependent upon the situation or the rank structure, there may be layers between you and the frontline that the bulk of those under you need to navigate before they speak with you directly. This is one of the realities of working in a para-military organization.)

In a broader sense, a Leader can Lead even those they've never met. Some of the people who have reached out to me, sight unseen, through reading my first book or through a social media post have incredible stories of redemption or heartbreak and everything in between. Quite often, these people are simply looking for a sympathetic ear who is willing to listen; other times they are rapidly spiraling like I did and are looking for some direction or suggestions how to stop the spiral. To be able to help these people, who may be half a world away, is both humbling and extremely gratifying.

What – the topics of conversation for a Leader are myriad. For purposes of this writing, we are sticking with conversations around difficult, personal topics. As stated earlier, sometimes Leaders must initiate conversations with those they Lead on issues like health, wellness, finances, changes in personality, decrease in work ability or ethic, and so on. These are all topics that many people will want to avoid regardless of what side of the desk they are on during the conversation. However, they can often prove to be among the most rewarding, life-altering discussions that an enlightened, authentic Leader can have. Due to their sensitive nature, the person in crisis will often not be willing to open the dialogue, leaving it to the Leader to do so – hence the need to know one's people and have empathy for what they are going through on a day-to-day basis.

Where – there is a very old saying in leadership circles: Praise in Public, Punish in Private. In other words, when you are giving your people kudos, make sure that you step back from the limelight and give them the credit they deserve as loudly as possible. On the other hand, if you must deal with disciplinary issues, you do so as subtly as possible, behind closed doors at a reasonable volume and tone. Discipline should never be meted out in front of other people who aren't directly involved.

(A side note – some leadership experts will argue that having a disciplinary discussion with someone in front of other members of your team can be a tactically sound move when it comes to issues that have impacted the whole team, especially if the person you're disciplining is the key 'agitator' who is poisoning the rest. This is a fine art, as while it can show that you are a Leader who is aware of what is going on, if handled wrong it can backfire in terms of turning the other team members against you, as well as potentially open you up for a complaint or grievance. Like with much of Leadership, this tactic is a tricky mix of art and science.)

In my experience, difficult conversations should be treated the same way - behind closed doors. Keep in mind that these discussions should NOT be disciplinary in nature unless the discipline is a natural outgrowth of the situation or vice versa (for example, an employee whose performance has visibly declined discloses to you that their spouse has left, or that they are having medical issues that are making it difficult to work at their regular level, etc.) The definition of 'closed door' is broad – it could be your office, an emergency vehicle at the side of the road, a quiet corner during a conference…. you simply should work with what you have at the time. Most people are more willing to open up on sensitive issues when they know that they are in a safe, secure environment where they can talk freely. If you as a Leader indicate that you are willing to listen and respond in a way that continues that safety and security, you have the groundwork laid for a meaningful conversation.

Some of the most meaningful talks I've ever had have been sitting in a cruiser with a partner, during a slow graveyard shift, when the world seems to be moving slower and the stars over the country road you're parked on seem to shine more brightly away from the lights of town. Breakthroughs, sharing, and compassion can take place anywhere.

When – This one is simple. The quicker the conversation is had after the crisis has arisen or you find out that there is an issue, the better. With a traumatic incident, for example, it has been proven over and over that the quicker the subject of the trauma begins talking to someone who will listen, the less the impact and the quicker the recovery. This also ties in with being the one who starts the ball rolling. As a Leader, being proactive, being the one who initiates a conversation that is likely to be unpleasant for one or both parties, can be an incredibly powerful tool. In my own case, I attempted to speak about how Mike's death was affecting me that night, within an hour of his death, but was soundly rebuffed by the officer who should have been my lifeline. Had he listened, had I been able to hear some sympathetic words, (and, quite frankly, if I had persisted in trying to find someone who would listen,) the way my life unfolded between 2004 and 2012 would have been very different.

Why – the point of communication is to bridge an interpersonal gap between a speaker and a listener(s). Generally, the speaker wants to convey some intent to the listener. Dependent on the speaker, the intent may be very easy to fathom, or it may be buried beneath layers of fluff.

Having been in thousands of both kinds of conversations as a Leader, I would argue that the more explicit approach is the simpler one – let the listener directly know your intent.

Sometimes, it is very easy to question why we must have these difficult conversations. If the routines of life and work are carrying on smoothly, why rock the boat? I remember when I had my first session with my psychologist, she presented me with a simple question: "Do you want to get back to the man; the dad; the father; the cop that you were? If you do, it will take work and I won't carry you."

I remember sitting and contemplating that for a good minute. Did I want to do that work? It would have been easy to continue being miserable and angry to those around me, and it wouldn't take any effort on my part. But then I remembered what Cathy said to me the night that I had my emotional and spiritual crash at the end of my downwards spiral: Get help or get out. That was pretty black and white.

The first formative steps to my recovery came about because of two difficult conversations: Cathy being so upfront about what she needed and my doctor being so blunt and honest about what therapy with her would mean.

If you have moved into a leadership position, my hope is that you want to be a Leader as opposed to a leader. If that is the case, then the argument becomes simple: Leaders care. About their people. Their operations. Their team. Their own health and wellness. If you care, then you have an obligation to initiate these conversations, for the good of all those things I just named.

How – The how of difficult conversations is potentially the most crucial factor. The approach that you take to what could potentially be a life-altering conversation will make or break how that conversation unfolds.

Conversations and communications are a constant, ongoing, evolving cycle:

-Speaker conveys an intent to the listener.

-There is an impact on the listener that causes them to react.

-The speaker assesses the reaction of the listener.

-The speaker re-conveys the original intent (with a new approach, if needed) or expresses a new intent.

And the cycle continues until a (hopefully) meaningful conversation with understanding on both sides has been had.

As a Leader, you should be naturally empathetic. That's a good start. Real empathy will show through in your discussion. I have found that, when trying to open a conversation, sharing a piece of your own story that relates to the current situation or making an admission of your own is a very strong way to start (remember that piece about being open and authentic?) Showing vulnerability opens doors to sharing and questions about even the most sensitive of issues.

Conversely, even the least imaginative person can surely envision how a conversation about, say, a mental health issue could go with a HR manager who does just that – manage as opposed to Lead. If your only consideration is the benefit to your company or your organization, if you see people simply as assets, then that will be your focus, and it will show, no matter how sincere of a face you put on. A Leader will find a way to explore the issue and be able to articulate how the crisis they are helping someone with will have an impact on both the person and the organization and how the impacts are interconnected. If you take care of the person and their issues, you are doing long-term repairs that can't help but ultimately benefit everyone.

> **"Whatever words we utter should be chosen with care for people will hear them and be influenced by them for good or ill."**
>
> —BUDDHA, TEACHER, SAGE, POET, FOUNDER OF BUDDHISM

> **"The single biggest problem in communication is the illusion that it's taken place."**
>
> —GEORGE BERNARD SHAW, IRISH PLAYWRIGHT, AUTHOR, AND POLITICAL ACTIVIST

Retreat Is a Viable Strategy

Once you start something, don't stop until someone who is better equipped than you to handle the situation takes over or you've exhausted all your energy, resources, and time. As a Leader, there is no shame in admitting that you have given your all to something but simply didn't possess everything it took to close the deal. True Leaders don't fear stepping back into the shadows and letting someone else take the spotlight.

Keep in mind, however, that stepping back is NOT the same as simply quitting in anger or frustration and possibly derailing the project. Making wise use of other members of your team who are better suited for situational leadership than you are is just that – wise. There is very little redemption in leading your team into a blind canyon with no exit when another leader may have known about a side passage that would have let you take another way out.

This point recalls, for me, the night Mike died. When he died in the van, I was getting ready to begin CPR. We had always been taught, once you start CPR, don't stop until you are either physically exhausted and can no longer continue, or someone with more knowledge, skills, and abilities arrives. At the time, I had no idea how long any backup or help would be, but I was ready to give it my damndest until I couldn't do so anymore.

But, even with that mindset, when I heard the paramedics clanking down the bank of the ditch behind me, I felt an incredible wave of relief wash over me and was happy to get the hell out of their way and let them do what they do.

> "He who advances without seeking fame, who retreats without escaping blame, he whose one aim is to protect his people and serve his Lord, that man is a Jewel of the Realm."
> -SUN TZU, 5TH CENTURY BC CHINESE GENERAL, MILITARY STRATEGIST, AND AUTHOR OF *THE ART OF WAR* (ONE OF MY FAVOURITE BOOKS AND ONE I REREAD EVERY YEAR)

> "Part of the happiness of life consists not in fighting battles, but in avoiding them. A masterly retreat is in itself a victory."
> -NORMAN VINCENT PEALE, AMERICAN MINISTER, SPEAKER, AND WRITER; AUTHOR OF 'THE POWER OF POSITIVE THINKING'

Lighten Your Load When You Can Do So

Capital-L leaders often carry extremely heavy burdens and a tremendous amount of stress. When someone who has your best interests at heart gives you a chance to talk and to unload some of that heaviness, do so. That's why it's so key that Leaders build a strong, stable support team around themselves.

I had the perfect opportunity to do that twelve hours after Mike's death when Cathy clearly recognized that something was wrong and that I wasn't myself. When she asked if I wanted to talk about my night, I turned her down. That is one of my everlasting regrets about my trauma journey; that I had a chance to minimize the damage so quickly after it happened and didn't take it. My pride, my ego, my inexperience, all got in the way of the tremendous possibility I had for some self-care and a check-in with someone who had a vested interest in my well-being.

Since then, I recognize that as a Leader you must take those opportunities as well as provide them. Cathy is a Capital-L Leader in her own right and was certainly equipped to help me start processing the experience, had I only let her try.

> **"Teach me to feel another's woe, to hide the fault I see, that mercy I to others show, that mercy show to me."**
>
> -Alexander Pope, English poet; best known for his satirical verse and his extensive translations of the works of Homer

> **"Surround yourself with good people.**
> **People who are going to be honest with you**
> **and look out for your best interests."**
>
> -Derek Jeter, 20-year New York Yankee shortstop, 5-time World Series Champion, part-owner, and CEO of the Miami Marlins

Self-Care Is Not Selfish, It's Survival

At times of crisis, keeping your mind and body focused and healthy is key. The connection between mind and body is long-established – good health in one creates a feedback loop of good health in the other. That's why it is so important to continue routines, especially those around health and wellness, when you find yourself in a crisis.

This is another mistake I made. During the times that I should have been using my fitness routines, proper nutrition, and meditation to stay focused and centered (the times right after Mike's death and during my downward spiral in 2011 most readily come to mind,) I completely abandoned them and started relying on junk food, caffeine, alcohol, TV, and video games. It was easier and much more comforting to use those crutches, but ultimately way more harmful.

Keeping that mental and physical edge is what marks you as a Leader; if you start to collapse, you lose your effectiveness. Role modelling a healthy mind-body connection is never a poor choice either.

Self-care is one of the cornerstones of speaking engagements done by Cathy and me. She is always sure to emphasize the crucial role that self-care plays for those taking care of and supporting someone else, and she will readily admit that if she were not watching out for her own health, wellness, and sanity during the deepest, darkest days of my PTS that our home life would have rapidly fallen apart.

> **"When the well's dry, we know the worth of water."**
> -BENJAMIN FRANKLIN, EARLY AMERICAN AUTHOR, POLITICIAN, SCIENTIST, INVENTOR, HUMORIST, CIVIC ACTIVIST, STATESMAN, AND DIPLOMAT; FOUNDING FATHER OF THE UNITED STATES

> **"If your compassion does not include yourself, it is incomplete."**
> -JACK KORNFIELD, AMERICAN AUTHOR, SPEAKER, AND TEACHER IN THE VIPASSANA SCHOOL OF AMERICAN THERAVADA BUDDHISM

Work Is Work, Not Life

As a Leader, work should never be your sole means of coping with the rest of your life. I went down that hole for years, using work, special assignments, and the possibility of promotion as my motivation.

And my escape.

I wore my job like a mask – at work I was calm, cool, and in charge. At home, that mask came off and I was an awful dad and husband. It was easier to be at work and to take refuge in my role and uniform.

After discovering that I had PTS, and when starting to rebuild, I had to learn a new part of Leadership – knowing how and when to keep work and home life separate. There are many ways to do this, dependent upon your role at work and what your responsibilities are: have a hard-cutoff time to leave work, shut off your technology at home, use your weekends and vacation time to separate yourself from work... Whatever it takes to create a disconnect between work and home.

(In my case, as I previously mentioned, my disconnect included approximately 18 months of medical leave starting in mid-2019, about a year after I completed the first edition of this book. It was time well spent and much needed.)

This issue is not uncommon. In my talks with hundreds of first responders dealing with PTS, the concept of using work as a mask came up over and over. The other recurring theme was that those who felt they experienced post-traumatic growth learned to clearly delineate work from home as a way of helping manage the impact of trauma on their lives.

As a Leader, don't let your realization that having clearly defined work and home lives is a necessity come from a traumatic incident.

> "It is better to rise from life as from a banquet - neither thirsty nor drunken."
>
> -ARISTOTLE, 3ʳᴰ CENTURY BC GREEK PHILOSOPHER, SCIENTIST, AND POET

> "Love those close to you: Failure of your company is not failure in life. Failure in your relationship is."
>
> -EVAN WILLIAMS, INTERNET ENTREPRENEUR AND CO-FOUNDER OF TWITTER

If There's No Way, Make One, and Leave a Trail for Others

Leaders are trailblazers. They willingly tackle the topics and issues many others shy away from. Leaders need to be bold. Leaders need to be brave.

This is endlessly important concerning mental health and psychological injuries. In today's climate, no matter the workplace, when it comes to mental health issues, only being a trailblazer will pull issues that have lain in the shadows for centuries out into the light of day, where they can wither and die.

If a resource, tool, or concept you need doesn't exist, create it. Leaders sometimes must be their own advocate, inventor, or project manager.

When I first put in a compensation claim for my PTS as a workplace injury, I found myself having to work within an archaic system that barely recognized the concept of psychological injuries. The amount of paperwork being requested was mind-boggling and there was very little in the way of support for completing the process.

It quickly became apparent that if I were going to get my claim honoured, I would have to dig in, fight for what I knew was mine and work the system to my advantage. It took two months, but I ended up completing the needed paperwork, keeping track of what I did along the way. Afterwards, I had a template in place, and was able to help almost twenty other officers put in their own injury claims over the next few years using my claim as a basis for success.

In 2016 the process for first responders to put in a psychological injury claim in the area I live became much easier, so the need to struggle through the system as I did has now been drastically minimized. This was a huge win for PTS advocacy groups, many of which I've had the pleasure to work alongside.

I found when I re-opened my claim for a psychological injury in 2019 that both the process and the machinery in place to support me outside of my employer had improved and smoothened substantially.

> "You can never cross the ocean unless you have the courage to lose sight of the shore."
>
> -CHRISTOPHER COLUMBUS, 15TH CENTURY ITALIAN EXPLORER AND NAVIGATOR; CREDITED WITH OPENING THE FIRST PERMANENT LINKS FROM EUROPE TO THE AMERICAS

> "A man who wants to lead the orchestra must turn his back on the crowd."
>
> -MAX LUCADO, AMERICAN PASTOR, AUTHOR, AND MOTIVATIONAL SPEAKER

One Person's Stress Is Another Person's Routine

This one is simple. Stress is relative. One person's worst day ever is another's average day at the office.

I have an example of this I often use. In my career, I've stopped thousands of cars. Unless there is something unusual about the car or we have information that the car is stolen or something similar, stopping a car is a routine procedure for most cops. The officer approaches the car, interacts with the driver, asks for documentation, and proceeds to act based on the information the officer discovers. Although the officer always has a certain level of vigilance, most vehicle stops are simple and over in a matter of minutes. It's just part of a cop's average day.

However…

For the person being stopped, that stop could literally be the most stressful thing that ever happened to them. Most people are anxious when they get stopped by the police; in this case I'm not talking about them.

I'm talking about the people whose heart rate and respiration go up, who hyperventilate, who cry (and, trust me, we can tell the difference between real tears and crocodile tears during a stop,) who become incapable of giving us answers to even the simplest question. Their fight or flight response has been activated.

If the person is wanted or is a suspended driver, this is often the point where they will flee, or, in extreme circumstances, start planning to attack the officer. If they're everyday Joe or Jane citizen, they'll simply sit there awaiting their fate, anxious and sweaty. Most of the time, the driver will get a ticket and be on their way (occasionally, there will be an arrest or other interaction, of course,) usually after a few minutes spent composing themselves. The officer will make some notes, clear the stop, and be on their way as well.

For one of the parties, it was just part of the duties of the day. For the other, it was possibly their first interaction ever with a police officer and a reminder that there are societal expectations of safe driving, laws to reinforce those expectations, and penalties for not doing so.

Other factors can create even more of an impact. Policing in North America has gone through a reckoning in the last few years, and the level of trust and support that policing previously enjoyed in many sectors has waned.

Since 2015, North America has experienced a surge of immigration. Many of these newcomers hail from areas where dealing with the police is a terrifying prospect – corruption, assault, torture, rape, even murder are common offshoots of dealing with police in these under-developed and war-torn areas of the world. People with strong anti-law enforcement or anti-government stances may resent the fact that they are being stopped by an officer and immediately escalate the confrontation. The driver or a passenger in the vehicle may be in medical distress, which is why the driver was speeding.

Leaders will inevitably find themselves in these types of situations; the key is to recognize that the person you are dealing with is at an escalated level of stress. As a Leader, part of your role is to reduce the stress imbalance to help the person you're dealing with, whether a member of the public or a member of your team. There are many ways to do this, but I would argue that the simplest is through conversation. Have a reasonable, rational, calming conversation with the person to help set their mind at ease and assure them that you understand how anxious they currently are.

Once you're on a more even footing with your respective stress levels, you should find that the conversation can proceed more smoothly and ultimately be more productive.

> "If you really want to escape the things that harass you, what you're needing is not to be in a different place but to be a different person."
>
> —SENECA, ROMAN WRITER, PHILOSOPHER, AND RHETORICIAN

> "In times of stress, the best thing we can do for each other is to listen with our ears and our hearts and to be assured that our questions are just as important as our answers."
>
> —FRED (MISTER) ROGERS, BELOVED CHILDREN'S ENTERTAINER AND SWEATER AFICIONADO

Be Wise in the Use of Your Resources, Just Like the Scout Motto Says

Leaders take advantages of all the resources at their disposal. It doesn't matter whether you're acting in your role as an incident commander, balancing work and home, walking a team member through a crisis, or looking after your own health and wellness. The world is full of tricks, hacks, and tips that you can add to your Leadership toolkit, tucked away waiting for the perfect opportunity to save the day.

Leaders will naturally fill their toolkit whenever possible – being mentored by other Leaders, taking training, mentoring others, and learning from mistakes. Using the tools you have available, especially if some of these tools are much more knowledgeable than you (I'm thinking, for example, of specialized law enforcement units who can be called on to respond to incidents they are uniquely suited for,) is smart Leadership.

I've heard leaders say that they would prefer to call every shot themselves, regardless of what those around them advise, and that to do otherwise is 'passing the buck'. Capital-L Leaders understand that taking the counsel of those who know best is not by any means passing the buck – you are still responsible for the decisions that are made; now, however, you're doing so while better armed with knowledge and opinions.

This also includes knowing the resources that are available to you and your people with regards to their health, wellness, and fitness – Leaders should have an excellent grasp of internal and external resources that can be accessed in times of crisis and to build resiliency.

Once I was diagnosed with PTS, and finally realized what I was dealing with, Cathy and I started circling the wagons and lining up the things we would need to take on this fight together.

I reached out to my family doctor, who was 500 kilometers away yet still talked me through the initial shock of realizing just how far I had fallen. I spoke with close friends in their peer support capacity to get some guidance and to hear what I had told dozens of officers myself over and over – that I wasn't alone, that it wasn't the end, that I would get through this. I opened up to my brand-new supervisor, hoping for understanding and empathy, which I got in spades. I consulted with our internal employee assistance program and spoke with my Association (union) representative. I knew I needed a psychologist, and literally picked a name at random from a list that my employer provided me with. I didn't know who I was getting; I just knew that I was going to start getting professional help. All small steps that together added up to a formidable offensive against this monster in my life that I finally had a name for, PTS.

As I've already alluded to, Cathy was truly the Leader at this time. She kept me going most days, even when I couldn't imagine getting out of bed much less functioning. It was her who made appointments and helped me keep them straight, it was her who made sure I was eating properly, it was her who kept the normalcy of the house going, it was her who ultimately was a much better person than I could ever hope to be, who stuck with me even though I was putting her and our marriage through hell, and who decided that she was going to do everything possible to make sure that we remained a family.

When I think about those who are less fortunate than I, who are homeless, jobless, living on the streets, all while dealing with psychological issues, it boggles me that there are still those among that population who rise above their circumstances and come back to the person they used to be.

Family was a resource that, at the time, I squandered. I will never do so again.

> **"A fool despises good counsel, but a wise man takes it to heart."**
>
> -CONFUCIUS, 6TH CENTURY BC CHINESE TEACHER, POLITICIAN, AND PHILOSOPHER

> **"Start where you are. Use what you have. Do what you can."**
>
> -ARTHUR ASHE, AMERICAN PROFESSIONAL TENNIS PLAYER; WON THREE GRAND SLAM TITLES; FIRST BLACK PLAYER SELECTED TO THE UNITED STATES DAVIS CUP TEAM; ONLY BLACK MAN EVER TO WIN THE SINGLES TITLE AT WIMBLEDON, THE US OPEN, AND THE AUSTRALIAN OPEN

Take Shelter in the Harbour of Your Family

Which leads perfectly into my next point: let your family be your rock during times of crisis.

For the better part of a decade, I did the exact opposite. I viewed my issues as exactly that – *my* issues. I forgot one of the most important parts of being in a family – when you have family, you don't exist in a silo. Your life is irrevocably intertwined with those people, both the family you are born into and the one that you develop as you go through life.

'Family' as a term has a very broad definition and can include virtually anyone you wish. I know in the emergency response field, we often refer to those we work with as family, which, considering how much time we spend with them, is accurate.

I didn't let *any* of my family in, be they work or home. In hindsight, that ranks among the larger mistakes I made of many.

I had people both at home and at work who could have anchored me, supported me, kept me steady and on course when it started to become more and more apparent that something was wrong as I slipped further down the rabbit hole to my inevitable crash.

Let your family in during times of crisis – you won't regret it. They'll probably already know something is wrong anyways.

> **"In time of test, family is best."**
> -Burmese proverb, author unknown

> **"You know, all that really matters is that the people you love are happy and healthy. Everything else is just sprinkles on the sundae."**
> -Paul Walker, American actor, star of Fast and Furious series; died at age **40** in a racecar crash

Prepare for Monday Morning Quarterbacking

It is inevitable that as a Leader, you will be challenged. Your decisions will be questioned, both to your face and behind your back. Your actions will be watched, scrutinized, and dissected endlessly. Quite often, a decision that you have minutes or seconds to make will be taken apart by those with the luxury of time on their hands.

This has happened to me more times than I can count, sometimes respectfully, sometimes in the heat of crisis. Have I always made the correct decision? No, but in looking back I will forever stand behind the fact that I made a decision at a time when someone had to.

One interesting offshoot of this point. Since I am very open about my PTS, while continuing in a Leadership role, I have been asked several times if the trauma has impacted my decision-making. My answer is always 'Yes, how could it not?'

By that, I don't mean that I'm shying away from conflict or crisis or the possibility that myself or someone else could become traumatized – as first responders, we don't have the choice of picking and choosing what calls we respond to.

What I mean is that I'm now more careful, more cautious. More willing to consider opinions aside from my own and more appreciative of those around me who provide those opinions. I'm certainly more cognizant of the psychological and physical impact that work can have on myself, and my team, and I make sure that at the end of the day, all the supports possible have been put into place.

I have also become much more aware of issues that I used to take for granted as simply part of society, like substance use, homelessness, and the prevalence of mental health issues in society. Once you've been part of those problems, it's hard not to have a changed perspective.

The ultimate point of the preceding is this: it doesn't matter what other people think of you if you can look in the mirror and sleep at night, knowing that you have done everything you can (to the best of your ability and with the tools at your disposal) to get everyone home safely at the end of the day.

"It is not the critic who counts; not the man who points out how the strong man stumbles, or where the doer of deeds could have done them better. The credit belongs to the man who is actually in the arena, whose face is marred by dust and sweat and blood; who strives valiantly; who errs, who comes short again and again, because there is no effort without error and shortcoming; but who does actually strive to do the deeds; who knows great enthusiasms, the great devotions; who spends himself in a worthy cause; who at the best knows in the end the triumph of high achievement, and who at the worst, if he fails, at least fails while daring greatly, so that his place shall never be with those cold and timid souls who neither know victory nor defeat."

- THEODORE ROOSEVELT, 26TH PRESIDENT OF THE UNITED STATES, AUTHOR, EXPLORER, SOLDIER, NATURALIST

"Common sense is the Monday morning quarterback who could have won the ball game if he had been on the team. But he never is. He's high up in the stands with a flask on his hip."

-RAYMOND CHANDLER, AMERICAN AUTHOR, AND SCREENWRITER

Sometimes You Have to Bet Heavy When the Odds Are Against You

There are times in life that, for the greater good, you must put your foot down, risk it all, and do something that may end up terribly painful for everyone involved. I mentioned earlier that in the early days of my PTS diagnosis, Cathy was the true Leader in our house. This included making some very tough decisions necessary for the survival and well-being of our family and each other.

At one point, her stance was a simple one – get help, or get out. She was no longer willing to live with my anger, with my being withdrawn and walled off from everyone else, with my disrespect of our marriage and the threat it presented to our kids.

She knew instinctively what had to be done to secure a future for all of us and did it.

It was a scenario that could have ended very differently. If I had refused to get help, refused to change, Cathy very likely would have left me and taken Jack and Brady with her. It would have been devastating financially, emotionally, and psychologically for all concerned.

Regardless of that, she knew what had to happen and was willing to risk that painful outcome to attain what she knew would be beneficial in the long run – she would either be rid of a husband who was impeding healthy growth for her and her kids, or I would get the help she insisted on, and she would get her husband back.

It was the perfect definition of tough love, and, although at first, I felt like my hand was forced, I've since come to see that what she did was the ultimate act of love – she was risking upheaving her whole life in a last-ditch effort to get me back to the man I used to be.

If you are lucky enough to be a Leader with someone in your life who cares that deeply for you, take that tough love when it's offered and hold onto it with both hands.

> "Success is not measured by what you accomplish, but by the opposition you have encountered, and the courage with which you have maintained the struggle against overwhelming odds."
>
> -ORISON SWETT MARDEN, AUTHOR AND ONE OF THE EARLIEST AMERICAN MOTIVATIONAL SPEAKERS

> "When something is important enough, you do it even if the odds aren't in your favour."
>
> -ELON MUSK, SOUTH AFRICAN / CANADIAN ENTREPRENEUR, ENGINEER, INVENTOR; INITIAL INVESTOR IN SPACEX, PAYPAL, AND TESLA AUTOMOTIVE

You Will Make Mistakes – Own Them

When the time comes, a Leader will own their mistakes. They are, after all, your mistakes. It's far too easy to blame other aspects of your organization or team – a lack of communication, misunderstood directions, laziness on the part of a member, budget issues.... when it comes to blame, the sky can be the limit. A true Leader will step up and admit when they've made a mistake.

I have one painful lesson to add to this: don't expect those with less developed leadership to go to bat for you when the chips are down if it could mean difficulties for them. Not everyone is a Leader, that is a simple fact of life. There are many people content to go through life like they're covered in Teflon, hoping that nothing sticks to them and that eventually the problem will go away or move on to the next involved party.

Shortly after my PTS diagnosis in 2012, there was one bright spot. I earned a promotion into a role which I had been eyeing for years. I did some initial training, was given a certificate of promotion, even got fitted for new uniforms. It was a very happy few weeks.

Until the bottom dropped out.

One day, I was told that there had been a complaint lodged against me internally. Without going into a ton of detail, I had made an admittedly very stupid remark at a social event that obviously hurt someone deeply. I apologized and did what I could to minimize the damage, but, inevitably, I was dragged into a complaint process. One of the things I had been counting on was for some previous co-workers to assist the investigators by helping set up some context for the situation. After a few weeks of investigation, the complaint was substantiated, and when I read the report I found, to my dismay, that none of the people I hoped would be able to assist me did so. They all denied or downplayed the information I had assumed they were going to be able to provide to the investigators.

At first, I was extremely upset at this. I lost the promotion and job I wanted, and I laid a large part of the blame on those I felt let me down. After a few months of reflecting, however, I realized that my mindset was wrong. I had made the mistake, not them. Not everyone is willing to step forward and support an unpopular cause, and it appeared at that point that I was as unpopular a cause as you could find. As a Leader I needed to step up, admit that I had made a stupid, mindless mistake, and move on. It hurt, but painful lessons are often the best teachers.

A corollary to this – it's also important to know when standing your ground and fighting the battle isn't worth the possible collateral damage, even if winning is a distinct possibility. Several people said that I should fight this process, that I could take it to a formal hearing, call witnesses, and plead my case more fully.

But to what end? A Pyrrhic victory? Dragging all involved through a hearing process that could stretch out over months or years? Fighting for a position that, even had I gotten it, would already be tainted (and myself tainted as a Leader) because of how my success in getting it came about?

No, it wasn't worth it. I took my lumps, publicly admitted my mistake and that I wasn't getting the position after all and moved on.

Sometimes, you must ask yourself how badly you need to be right.

In the long run, people whose opinion I trust immensely told me that I had come out of the whole ordeal with a measure of respect for how I had handled things and that, at least as far as they had heard, people's impression of me hadn't suffered too much. That's what comes from living life as a Leader.

This was ultimately a blessing in disguise. Not getting that position caused me to start reflecting on my career and where it was at. It made me realize that I truly didn't want to keep climbing; in fact, I was ready to simplify things. That's what led to my taking a step backwards in rank, moving the family back towards our hometowns, and remembering why I wanted to become a cop in the first place.

The universe works in funny ways.

> "If anyone can refute me – show me I'm making a mistake or looking at things from the wrong perspective, I gladly change. It's the truth I'm after, and the truth never harmed anyone. What harms us is to persist in self-deceit and ignorance."
>
> -Marcus Aurelius, 1st century Roman emperor, philosopher, and Stoicist; the last of the Five Good Emperors of Rome

> "You have to own your mistakes; otherwise your mistakes own you."
>
> -Paulo Coelho, Brazilian author, lyricist, and activist

Every Pilgrimage Has Rest Stops

Constant forward movement isn't always the best course of action. A Leader will realize when it's time to regroup and recharge. It could be a simple break, like vacation time, or something more complicated like a sabbatical or long-term medical leave. It's a must that you listen to your body and mind, process what they're telling you, and, if the message is that it's time for a break, then follow through and do what they're saying. Know when it's time to swallow your pride, take a step back, and regroup.

Notice, however, I didn't say that you should stop the journey forward. That journey should never stop…just have a detour every now and then.

I did this a few times, with major life moves, and I am better off for having done so:

When I started my PTS treatment in 2012, I was adamant that I continue working and maintain as much normalcy as possible. As I got a few months into the treatment, however, it readily became apparent that to properly tackle this thing I would need some time away from work. At first, I felt like this was a step backwards. As I moved into this time off, however, I began to realize that the break away from work, which, with the help of my doctor, was carefully structured to be productive and healthy, was a very tactically sound move. It let me focus on myself and the family without the added pressure that I dealt with on a day-to-day basis at the office. It also let me informally mentor the officer who was replacing me, so even in that time away I could still act as the Leader I wanted to continue being.

When I returned to work after that leave, I was refreshed, revitalized, and felt more in control of myself both as a police officer and a person. I honestly can't say that if I had continued working through that time that it wouldn't have had some long-lasting negative impact on either my career or my home life. That short separation from work was a much-needed step in my PTS journey and one that I now recommend to anyone who approaches me to ask about taking their own initial steps down the path to recovery.

In 2013, I gave up the position, the rank, and the salary I had climbed to because, ultimately, none of those things were helping me reach the goal I really needed to, which was to make my family feel safe and secure. This meant leaving life in a big city, moving to a smaller town closer to our families, and starting a new position that was getting me back to front-line policing after many years of sitting at a desk. It would ultimately be the best career move I ever made, but at the time it was a very humbling experience to give up so much when I had accomplished so many career milestones in such a brief time.

In 2018, I felt ready to resume more advanced duties and start to move back up that ladder, so I applied for a promotion and received it, getting a whole new set of responsibilities and a brand-new team to work with.

Then there was the 2019 leave I discussed earlier, which was essential to my health and wellness at that time.

One caveat that I do need to mention – the option to step back from things is extremely situational and is one that will take a fair amount of self-reflection. If you're dealing with a health issue, then I would also highly suggest that your medical professional be part of the decision as well.

Capital-L Leadership means knowing when you need to move off the frontlines and let someone else hold the reins, and there is no shame in doing so.

> "If you have no time to rest, its exactly the right time."
> -MARK TWAIN, AMERICAN HUMORIST, WRITER, EDITOR, AND LECTURER

> "If life is a journey, time should pull over at a rest stop sometimes – we should all be given a chance to get off and stretch our legs, collect our thoughts and reorganize."
> -ROB PAYNE, CANADIAN AUTHOR, EDITOR, AND NEWSPAPER CONTRIBUTOR

When the Universe Knocks, Open the Door

If you want to make a deep impression with your ideas and concepts, strike while the iron is hot. Sometimes, external factors that you never anticipated arise out of nowhere and provide you with the ideal opportunity to start a project, publish an article, or make your presence known. Leaders know that sometimes luck has a role to play – the key is to recognize when that door is open and how to go through it.

I'll elaborate on an experience of my own that I've already mentioned, the email I sent out detailing my PTS story.

In October of 2012, the Ombudsman of the province of Ontario released a report on how psychological injuries in police officers were being dealt with by police agencies. The report was not very positive and concluded that the needs of police officers dealing with operational stress injuries were, for the most part, not being met. On the day of the report's release, I was overseeing my work location, and was one of the recipients of an email from our command staff asking us to share the link to the online report and to discuss the issue with our officers.

I decided to do one better and took this opportunity to compose and send the email about my own experiences, starting with Mike's death and ending with sending the message as my first public revelation about dealing with post-traumatic stress.

It was no magnum opus; I simply laid out my story. But, coupled with the revelations of the Ombudsman's report as released that day, my message had an increased impact, and I reached many more people than I could have without the report being in the media and top of people's minds at that time.

As a result, I had dozens of first responders reach out to me asking for help, for suggestions, or just to chat. I have no idea how much help any of my responses were, but to have had the chance to offer them as a voice of experience was incredibly rewarding.

Capital-L Leadership sometimes needs a little nudge in the right direction from factors outside your control.

> **"The opportunity is often lost by deliberating."**
> -PUBLILIUS SYRUS, 1ST CENTURY SYRIAN/
> LATIN WRITER AND PHILOSOPHER

> **"When you walk up to opportunity's door, don't knock on it. Kick that bitch in, smile, and introduce yourself."**
> -DWAYNE 'THE ROCK' JOHNSON, WRESTLER,
> ACTOR, AND MENTAL HEALTH ADVOCATE

Reduction of Stress Is a Force Multiplier

This is an extremely simple concept, but one that many Leaders have trouble grasping, as they tend to take on more and more challenges and work. As you begin to lower the stress in your life, all your positive traits become more and more pronounced, you have time for activities more essential than worrying, and you open yourself up for richer and more diverse experiences.

There are so many ways to do this. Cut toxic people from your life, or, if you can't do that, minimize the power they have to impact you and your environment. Curtail your social media use or stop social media altogether. Say 'no' to projects that your heart isn't in. Don't read the comments for online news articles you're involved with. Assign two tasks a week to people you trust. Keep on top of your health and wellness. Pet your dogs. Whatever it is you do to lower your cortisol (bad hormones) and raise your endorphins (good hormones,) do it!

As you do this, I think you'll be stunned to see how many things that seem important on a day-to-day basis really aren't worth your time, and suddenly you'll have time for the more important, more meaningful activities that help you grow as a Leader.

"Our anxiety does not empty tomorrow of its sorrow, but only empties today of its strengths."
-CHARLES SPURGEON, ENGLISH PREACHER, AUTHOR, AND RELIGIOUS REFORMER

"Your calm mind is the ultimate weapon against your challenges. So relax."
-BRYAN MCGILL, THOUGHT LEADER, ACTIVIST, AUTHOR, AND SOCIAL ENTREPRENEUR

Strength of Spirit Boosts Strength of Leadership

Along with the body and mind, a Leader must nurture the spirit. I don't mean in a religious sense, as spirit is not simply adherence to a religious faith. Spirit has been defined and demonstrated for me as the inner you, the core of who are and what makes you tick, the qualities regarded as forming the definitive or typical elements in your character. In simplest terms, what makes you, you.

There are many ways to do this, more than I could ever articulate. You are probably already doing many of the necessary things without knowing it – if something makes you happy, it's feeding the spirit!

If you would like to take this to another level, there are many self-guided meditations and breathing exercises designed to help you explore your spiritual side easily available online.

There are also full retreats and training programs that will help do the same. I would like to put in a plug for one that did incredible things for Cathy and me, the Hoffman Institute program (hoffmaninstitute.ca). I don't want to say much for fear of spoiling it; suffice to say that it was a one-week, life-altering experience for both of us.

I attended a first responder / veteran retreat called Save A Warrior in 2019 that was yet another turning point in my life and my recovery. I spent a week exorcising more demons, many of them permanently, and filled a whole new toolkit with ways to cope, reflect, grow, and Lead.

When you make time to take care of your inner self, you're completing a triangle of 'you': mind, body, and spirit. Triangles are the most stable shape in nature. Coincidence?

> "Where the spirit does not work with the hand, there is no art."
>
> -LEONARDO DA VINCI, ITALIAN RENAISSANCE POLYMATH; AREAS OF INTEREST INCLUDED INVENTION, PAINTING, SCULPTING, ARCHITECTURE, SCIENCE, MUSIC, MATHEMATICS, ENGINEERING, LITERATURE, ANATOMY, GEOLOGY, ASTRONOMY, BOTANY, WRITING, HISTORY, AND CARTOGRAPHY. GENERALLY CONSIDERED ONE OF HISTORY'S GREATEST MINDS.

> "Each Warrior wants to leave the mark of his will, his signature, on important acts he touches. This is not the voice of ego but of the human spirit, rising up and declaring that it has something to contribute to the solution of the hardest problems, no matter how vexing!"
>
> -PAT RILEY, FORMER NBA COACH AND PLAYER; PRESIDENT OF THE MIAMI HEAT; 5-TIME NBA CHAMPIONSHIP COACH; 3-TIME NBA COACH OF THE YEAR; NAMED ONE OF 10 GREATEST COACHES IN NBA HISTORY

COVID

In the winter of 2019/2020, the world was introduced to the "severe acute respiratory syndrome coronavirus 2 (SARS-CoV-2), which became more familiarly became COVID-19 or COVID.

COVID completely changed how the whole world functioned – work, play, personal care, family dynamics, travel. It all changed, and likely forever.

For many people, during this time Leadership came to the forefront, either a lack of it or great examples of it.

People were working from home, away from their support systems and supervisory patterns. Did they have contact with their leadership, or were they left to drift on their own. Or was it somewhere in between.

Families were forced to put the critical care of loved ones into the hands of medical professionals who were working exhausted, drained, and emotional yet still expected to make life or death discussions or were separated for months on end because of medical restrictions.

Countless online and public battles were fought over masks and vaccines and somehow these things became politicized, partly leading to some of the most chaotic scenes ever seen in American politics.

I'm not going to talk about any of that.

I'm simply going to discuss what tools and techniques can be put into place when Leaders are faced with such a unique set of circumstances as what was thrust upon us by COVID.

Why did COVID hit so hard and necessitate the need for such a pivot in leadership? Well, a few reasons.

-extensive fear and stress caused by contact precautions, added workload of cleaning, disinfecting, wearing masks, and worries about contracting the disease in us and our families.

-added workload due to sickness and absences among places of employment and for many people a rapid shift to working from home or remotely.

-a blurring of lines between work and home, including the impact of taking care of sick family and home-schooling kids.

-uncertainty about what going back to work looks like.

-financial strain from shift or work changes as well as tremendous incidents of lost business, closed business, and accompanying financial worries.

-intense media, political, and social media pressure to have an opinion about COVID and all its spin-off impacts.

-constantly changing laws and guidelines about lockdowns, masks, public gatherings, etc.

-the ongoing need to isolate, limit social activities, loss of outlets like athletics and fitness, increased alcohol / drug consumption to cope.

-for Leaders, anxiety and frustration at not being able to support teams as normally done.

-an increase in the level of stress we were all feeling in general.

The great thing is that CAPITAL L Leadership lends itself to coping with the chaos that accompanies a massive disruption to our way of life. Each letter of the CAPITAL-L concept

-Communication – the people you lead need to know what is happening with their jobs and in their workplace and that they are not alone during this time of crisis and uncertainty. Constant communication will go a long way towards soothing fears of the unknown.

-Self-Awareness – as a Leader, you must be conscious of your own limitations, fears, needs, and goals while in the middle of a crisis. It's also extremely important to maintain distances and recognize the differences between your professional role and your personal role.

-Perspective – during times of crisis, Leaders must consider the myriad of things going on around them. For COVID, some things to consider include people working from home vs in the office, will your team be returning to a safe environment, and what changes have been made to routines that will be maintained. Keeping a broad perspective during these times will be of great benefit.

-Being an Island / Team Foundation – we've realized that it's important more than ever that you realize no one person can do everything needed on their own. If there is ever a time when you must rely on other team and family members, it's during a worldwide event like COVID. There is no shame at all in asking for, and taking, help.

-Admit Mistakes – COVID has been a completely new and uncharted situation. No one has made all the right moves – politicians, scientists, doctors, advisors, no one. The key with COVID, like with any time of trial, is to learn from those mistakes and not repeat them as cycles of the same situations continue.

-Live Out Loud / Leave A Trail – despite the chaos that COVID has caused, some amazing things have occurred. Communities came together to support frontline workers and developed a new understanding of frontline personnel and their challenges. Neighbours stepped up to check on each other and communities ran food drives and Christmas benefits for those who lost jobs or had to close their businesses. Families took time to slow down and re-think the constant noise and movement of life. People picked up new hobbies and caught up on reading and movies and became teachers and tutors for their kids. Opportunities absolutely do grow from chaos, if you are looking for the opportunities and willing to grab them even while you're in the middle of a storm.

"Be fast, have no regrets…If you need to be right before you move, you will never win."
    -MIKE RYAN, COVID EPIDEMIOLOGIST, WORLD HEALTH ORGANIZATION, ON HOW COUNTRIES THAT FARED THE BEST WITH COVID ACTED

"Be safe, be smart, be kind."
    -DR TEDROS GHEBREYESUS, DIRECTOR GENERAL, WORLD HEALTH ORGANIZATION, ON THE BEST WAY TO BEAT COVID

Faith Is a Powerful Weapon (But So Is Doubt)

As a Leader, you sometimes simply should have faith.

Faith that the people you are leading understand the situation that you are trying to lead them through.

Faith that the people around you understand that your open-door policy is exactly that.

Faith in the intelligence, courage, training, knowledge, skills, and abilities of those on your team.

Faith that, in a crisis, that team will take your direction to get the job done and then allow you to explain the whys and hows of the crisis after it's passed.

Faith that the public at large is starting to understand the impact of psychological injuries in the workplace and that this understanding will lead to more and more acceptance and assistance.

Finally, faith in yourself. This can often be the hardest one to hold onto. When you are striving to be the best Leader that you can be, the everyday obstacles and hurdles in your way can sometimes seem insurmountable. But they can be overcome and left behind as you continue down your life's path.

If anyone had told me ten years ago that I would once again be in control of my career; that I would have not one, but two books written about post-traumatic stress; that I would have moved back up the ranks again; and that I would have had the chance to tell my story to thousands of people, both through speaking engagements and through writing, I would have said that you should be committed. I could barely get out of bed some days – how the hell would I ever sit down and write a book or put my uniform back on again? At that time in my life, I had no faith, in myself or anyone else.

Yet here I sit looking the worst of my PTS in the rearview mirror and looking ahead to see what other side quests might be in store on this journey I find myself continuing. I know there will be more bumps in the road, more roadblocks. In fact, I'm counting on it.

But now I have faith in myself as a Capital-L Leader and faith in those closest to me; those who will be with me through good times and bad.

When you're a Leader, sometimes that's the only thing you need.

> **"We are twice armed when we fight with faith."**
> -Plato, 4th century Greek philosopher; student of Socrates and the teacher of Aristotle; generally considered one of the pivotal thinkers in the history of philosophy

"Believe in yourself! Have faith in your abilities! Without a humble but reasonable confidence in your own powers you cannot be successful or happy."

-NORMAN VINCENT PEALE, AMERICAN MINISTER, SPEAKER, AND WRITER; AUTHOR OF 'THE POWER OF POSITIVE THINKING'

Conclusion

Leadership isn't simple. If it was, then everyone would be a Leader. Or at least a leader.
There is an age-old debate over whether leaders are born or made. I don't think it's ever been definitively answered; there are very solid schools of thought on either side.

I am going to put forth my own theory, however. Capital-L Leaders are made from people who are already leaders. I don't particularly care how they became a leader in the first place; the key is that they have listened to and watched other Leaders, experienced working with Leaders, and nurtured the skills and traits that define Leaders.

    Empathy.
    Compassion.
    Resilience.
    Wisdom.
    Humour.

Responsiveness.
Action.
Discretion.
Honesty.
Confidence.
Creativity.
Loyalty.
Bravery.
Honour.

I take none of these words lightly. I've spent the last twenty-two years of my life working in a para-military organization, one steeped in tradition. I still believe that those words exist, that they mean something, and that they truly dictate what separates the wheat from the chaff.

During the final editing of the first edition of this book, I experienced something that, while not pleasant, reinforced many of the ideas that I wrote about in the book and listed in the previous paragraph.

On February 7, 2018, while responding to a motor vehicle collision on our largest highway on an extremely nasty winter day, I was hit by a truck. Not a transport truck, granted, it was 'only' a pickup. The exact sequence of events that led to me getting hit are too convoluted to recount here; the abridged version is that drivers who should have been watching what they were doing, driving the proper speed, and moving over away from my cruiser didn't do so, and as a result the passenger mirror of a pickup that drove the wrong way around my police car struck me across the chest and right shoulder. If I had been a foot further into the centre median, the truck would have hit me square with the grille and I have no doubt it would have killed me.

I'd been injured many times during my almost 20 years in policing, but without a doubt this was the most serious occurrence I'd been through. It resulted in an ambulance ride, a short hospital stay, ten days away from work, and lingering pain in my arm, chest, and shoulder when I exert myself too much.

It also resulted in two revelations.

The first was that after going through six years of recovery, and knowing what to expect after a traumatic incident, I was much better equipped to deal with the inevitable fallout. I had tips and tricks I could put into practice from the moment I was put into the ambulance to start minimizing the effects and magnitude of the trauma. When I had those recurring images of out-of-control transport trucks sliding towards me, I knew I had to tackle them head on, not push them to the back of my mind or pretend they weren't happening. When officers, doctors, and paramedics met me at the hospital, there was no hesitation to talk about what happened and what was going through my mind, because I now know that the sooner you start to talk about a traumatic incident the sooner you process it as real and the less your memory starts to distort or worsen the experience. When I saw Cathy and my boys peek around the curtains of my hospital bed, there were no secrets, no silence, no hiding of facts or feelings, because doing that before led me down that dark path that ended so terribly. When my oldest son, who held it all together the day I was hit to be a rock for his mom, came to me the next morning telling me that he was having trouble processing what happened and hadn't slept because he kept thinking about how I could have died, there was no downplaying the impact that my experience was having on my family, and we took steps to get him talking to someone as soon as possible about what he was experiencing.

The second revelation was this: change can indeed happen.

Starting the day I was injured, and in the days after, every single first responder I spoke with made it a point to mention not to return to duty until I was well in every capacity, including psychological. They may have put it diverse ways, and some more subtly than others, but the message was always there. This represented a far, far cry from Mike's death in 2004, when I was told to suck it up and that I had to toughen up if I wanted to be a leader, and an even further cry from the experiences of the old dogs around the various offices I've worked at who talked about being called every day by supervisors, asking when they were coming back to work.

It marked, in my mind, a huge change in mindset for the first responder community. Here were open, frank conversations about the necessity to make sure that what was between your ears was as healthy as the rest of the body before throwing yourself back into the fray. After spending the last six years fiercely advocating for more awareness and openness about PTS in the emergency services field, to see movement, to see progress, helped get me through the days when I was nursing torn muscles and moving through my house like an 80-year-old man.

I won't say that I'm glad that I was hit that day, but everything happens for a reason, and as I've alluded to a couple times now, the universe presents opportunities when and where they are meant to be. If nothing else, being injured allowed me to see, in action, the impact and effect that Leaders can have and to prove my axiom right: Capital-L Leaders see the people on their teams, and their well-being, as their most valuable asset.

Technology will continue to evolve as we slowly become a society that worries more about recording and broadcasting the acts of others than the morality of the acts themselves. Laws and governments will change. Society will continue to develop in some quarters, and regress in others. Politicians will keep doing what they do while the real machinery of the bureaucracy moves at its own pace.

Policing and the justice system will have to continue reckoning with changes that are in many cases long overdue, yet difficult to implement. Trust of those who protect and serve must, in many areas, need to be rebuilt. Those who take the oath, though, need to be supported and understood as we work to change ourselves; no one hates a bad cop more than a good cop.

The outrage of the week will continue. Celebrities will do stupid things be loved for it and regular people will make honest mistakes and get sacrificed on the altar of public opinion.

Professional athletes will keep making astronomical sums of money for running fast or skating hard or being able to catch a ball while the true heroes of society quietly go about their business of keeping the world safe and orderly. If COVID-19 showed us anything, it's that these quiet heroes truly make the world function.

Wars will keep happening. Terrorists will take lives premised on their god being better than any other gods. People who don't agree with the way the world is changing around them will buy weapons that they should never be able to get their hands on and wipe out innocents.

Masses of society will continue to be graded and classified by the colour of their skin or where they were born instead of the person that they are.

Before I started writing those last few paragraphs, I was going to simply say that the need for Leaders will never go away.

Then I read them again.

After re-reading them I think I must change my sentiment to 'We need Leaders more than ever.'

'Illegitimi non carborundum' (mock Latin) or 'Noli pati a scelestis opprimi' (real Latin) is a very elegant way of saying 'Don't let the bastards grind you down.'

Step beyond yourself and become the kind of Leader that the world will never stop needing.

> "Be the change you wish to see in the world."
>
> -MAHATMA GANDHI

> "Be the Leader that people want to see walk into the room, not out the door."
>
> -CHRIS LEWIS, OPP COMMISSIONER (RETIRED)

Resources

ORGANIZATIONS

Save-A-Warrior – saveawarrior.org

The Hoffman Process – hoffmaninstitute.ca or hoffmaninstitute.org

Wounded Warriors – woundedwarriors.ca

The Dad's Edge – group on Facebook

Reset Your Mindset – group on Facebook

BOOKS ON MENTAL HEALTH, LEADERSHIP, AND INSPIRATION – all available on Amazon

Unf*ck Yourself **and** Stop Doing That Sh*t – Gary John Bishop

The Secret Hero – Rhonda Byrne

Rising Above a Toxic Workplace – Chapman, White, and Myra

The Resilient Mind - Brad Coulbeck

The Dad's Edge – Larry Hagner

Save-My-Life School – Natalie Harris

Think and Grow Rich – Napoleon Hill

Never Stop On a Hill – Chris Lewis

The 21 Irrefutable Laws of Leadership – John Maxwell

The Book of Five Rings – Miyamoto Musashi

If the Brain Could Stop What the Eyes Have Seen – Marcie Resendes

Extreme Ownership – Jocko Willink and Leif Babin

Redefining Success – W. Brett Wilson

Star Wars Thrawn **and** Star Wars Thrawn Alliances – Timothy Zahn

POINTS FOR PONDERING

GENERAL

When you started reading this book, what was your definition of a leader?
Has it changed after finishing your read?
Were you surprised that it changed?

COMMUNICATION

What is your current style of communication? Do you think it will change based on using the 5 Ws and 1 H in the Communication section?
Think back on a difficult conversation you've had in your professional career or personal life. What new tools could you bring to that discussion from the CAPITAL-L toolkit?

SELF-AWARENESS

What is your definition of resilience?
Picture your resilience as a suit of armour – head, chest, arms, legs. What are your six pieces of armour – six tools you can call on in your life to help protect you and keep you standing when life gets difficult?
Consider a time you didn't succeed at something. In hindsight, what growth or learning did you ultimately experience?
Can you list five things you do for yourself on a regular basis? If not, you're not doing enough for your own well-being!

PERSPECTIVE

Think back to a time that you know you made a snap judgement before you had all the facts or based on your own perceptions. What ultimately happened and what would you do differently now?
Remember a time that you wish you had stopped your course of action to take a step back and re-evaluate. What was the impact? What difference would stopping to take that 'breath' make?

NO ONE IS AN ISLAND

Consider a recent time you knew you were in overwhelm. What are three things you could have done to offload some of your burden?
Reflect on your own experiences with mentoring, on either side of the equation. How did these experiences shape you?
Think of someone in your professional life who believes they warrant respect because of what they are, not who. What is your impression of that person and how do you avoid becoming them?

YOUR TEAM IS YOUR FOUNDATION

Think back to a situation that you wish you had more leadership during a personal or professional crisis. What difference would that extra leadership have made to you? To your team?

ADMITTING YOUR MISTAKES

Reflect on a time you owned a mistake, or a time that you wish you had owned a mistake you made. What was the damage cost of this mistake to you? To your team?

Are you holding a grudge due to a mistake someone made that deeply hurt you? Is carrying that grudge doing anything for you as a Leader or person? If you apply CAPITAL-L principles, can you start turning your mind to forgiving that person?

LIVING OUT LOUD

Think back to a time that you did something that terrified you but had a fantastic outcome. How did doing this change you?

Now think of a time that you wished you had taken a chance and would love a 'do over.' Are you carrying regrets because of this? How could you start to remedy the regret?

Can you recall a time that your journey of growth was helped by something outside of your control – luck, chance, fate, call it what you will. Did someone seem to come into your life at exactly the right time? Were you putting out to the universe that you were ready for someone or something to cross paths with you?

LEAVING A LEGACY

Think about a Leader in your own life who has left a trail for you to follow. How did you take that trail and start to make it your own?

When you die, there is always a dash between your date of birth and date of death. Your life is that dash. What do you want people to remember about your dash? If you don't like your dash right now, what steps do you have to take to create the legacy you want?

About The Author

Brian is a veteran police officer, retired lawyer, speaker, and author involved in the justice system since 1994. In 2004 he was the lead investigator in a motor vehicle crash involving the death of a close friend, causing his life to spiral until he was finally diagnosed with, and began therapy for, PTSD in 2012.

Brian published a book about his journey through his trauma, 'On the Other Side of Broken – One Cop's Battle With the Demons of PTSD' in 2016. The feedback from that book led to writing 'Career Suicide is Overrated' in 2018. He is also a freelance writer for outlets including Vocal and WhatCulture.

He is the creator the CAPITAL L Leadership training program and facilitates Mastermind groups and training sessions exploring the CAPITAL L Leadership concepts for modern professionals. The CAPITAL L Leadership program received the 2019 Corporate Livewire Award for Excellence in Mental Health Support. Brian speaks and consults for media outlets on issues surrounding trauma, leadership, and public safety across North America.

Brian is a graduate of the Queen's University Workplace Mental Health Leadership Certificate program, a certified leadership coach, a mindfulness coach, a critical incident stress supporter, and a member of the International Institute for Mental Health Leadership.

CONTACT INFORMATION

Website
www.brianknowler.com

Email
brian@knowlerconsulting.com

Professional Profile
linkedin.com/in/knowlerconsulting/

DID YOU ENJOY LEARNING THE PRINCIPLES OF CAPITAL-L LEADERSHIP?
THE BOOK IS ONLY THE BEGINNING

Knowler Consulting offers a full-range of programming and supporting materials to help you further your CAPITAL-L journey!

- CAPITAL-L Workbooks and Study Guides
- Single or multi-day training seminars for CAPITAL-L principles
- Ten-week Mastermind programs with other Leaders
- Individual and group CAPITAL-L coaching
- Media appearances by Brian and Cathy
- Blog entries

All available at brianknowler.com

www.ingramcontent.com/pod-product-compliance
Lightning Source LLC
LaVergne TN
LVHW011710060526
838200LV00051B/2838